The
BIBLE
Promise
Book®

*500 Scriptures
to Grow Your
Prayer Life*

The BIBLE Promise Book®

500 Scriptures to Grow Your Prayer Life

Written and Compiled by
Emily Biggers

BARBOUR BOOKS
An Imprint of Barbour Publishing, Inc.

Published by Barbour Books, an imprint of Barbour Publishing, Inc., 1810 Barbour Drive, Uhrichsville, Ohio 44683, www.barbourbooks.com

Our mission is to inspire the world with the life-changing message of the Bible.

Member of the
Evangelical Christian
Publishers Association

Printed in the United States of America.

Contents

1. What Is Prayer? 7
2. What Prayer Is Not 11
3. Why Should You Pray? 15
4. When Should You Pray? 19
5. Types of Prayer 23
6. Prayers of the Bible 27
7. The Lord's Prayer. 31
8. God Answers Prayers 35
9. Praying for Peace. 39
10. Praying for Direction 43
11. Praying for Assurance of Salvation. 47
12. Praying for Wisdom 51
13. Praying for Missionaries 55
14. Intercessory Prayer 59
15. The Power of Prayer 63
16. Praying as Jesus Prayed 67
17. Praying When Worried 71
18. Praying in the Spirit. 75
19. Praying for Children 79
20. Praying Scripture. 83
21. Praying the Psalms 87
22. Praying in the Morning 91
23. Praying Earnestly. 95
24. Praying Together 99
25. Praying Privately 103

26. Praying for God's Will 107

27. Praying the Names and Attributes of God . . . 111

28. Prayers for Strength. 115

29. Prayers for Healing 119

30. Prayers for Protection 123

31. Prayers for Courage. 127

32. Prayers of Confession 131

33. Paul's Prayers. 135

34. Prayers of Thankfulness. 139

35. Listening to God 143

36. Praying for Spiritual Growth 147

37. Prayers of Praise 151

38. Prayers for Boldness to Share the Gospel 155

39. Prayers for Heart Transformation. 159

40. Pray without Pretense 163

41. Pray Unceasingly. 167

42. Prayers of Spiritual Warfare 171

43. Prayers for the Lost 175

44. Prayers of Supplication 179

45. Praying for My Own Needs 183

46. Praying for Enemies 187

47. Praying through Trials 191

48. Problems in Prayer 195

49. Prayers for Deliverance 199

50. Praying for Miracles. 203

WHAT IS PRAYER?

Heavenly Father, I truly want to pray. I know prayer is important, and I have seen and heard of its power. But sometimes I don't know where to begin. There are so many needs around me that I feel overwhelmed. How could I possibly ask You to address all of them? I wonder if You are too busy handling more important requests than mine. And I often lose my train of thought and get distracted when I pray. Help me to understand what prayer is and how to grow in my prayer life. In Jesus' name I pray, amen.

1.

And it came to pass, that, as he was praying in a certain place, when he ceased, one of his disciples said unto him, Lord, teach us to pray, as John also taught his disciples.

LUKE 11:1

2.

But thou, when thou prayest, enter into thy closet, and when thou hast shut thy door, pray to thy Father which is in secret; and thy Father which seeth in secret shall reward thee openly.

MATTHEW 6:6

3.

But when ye pray, use not vain repetitions, as
the heathen do: for they think that they shall be
heard for their much speaking. Be not ye therefore like unto them: for your Father knoweth
what things ye have need of, before ye ask him.

MATTHEW 6:7–8

4.

And this is the confidence that we have in him,
that, if we ask any thing according to his will,
he heareth us: And if we know that he hear us,
whatsoever we ask, we know that we have
the petitions that we desired of him.

1 JOHN 5:14–15

5.

Seek the LORD and his strength,
seek his face continually.

1 CHRONICLES 16:11

6.

Praying always with all prayer and supplication
in the Spirit, and watching thereunto with all
perseverance and supplication for all saints.

EPHESIANS 6:18

7.

Then shall ye call upon me, and ye shall go and
pray unto me, and I will hearken unto you.

JEREMIAH 29:12

8.

If my people, which are called by my name,
shall humble themselves, and pray, and seek
my face, and turn from their wicked ways;
then will I hear from heaven, and will forgive
their sin, and will heal their land.

2 CHRONICLES 7:14

9.

I have called upon thee, for thou
wilt hear me, O God: incline thine
ear unto me, and hear my speech.

PSALM 17:6

10.

Likewise the Spirit also helpeth our infirmities:
for we know not what we should pray for as we
ought: but the Spirit itself maketh intercession
for us with groanings which cannot be uttered.

ROMANS 8:26

WHAT PRAYER IS NOT

Lord, in Your Word, I read about the Pharisees and others whose prayers were not pleasing to You. I must admit that I see a reflection of myself in their stories. Please help me to be humble in my prayers. Show me what prayer isn't so that my prayers will please You. I don't want anything to keep my prayers from being heard by You, Almighty God. In Jesus' name I pray, amen.

11.

And when thou prayest, thou shalt not be
as the hypocrites are: for they love to pray
standing in the synagogues and in the corners
of the streets, that they may be seen of men.
Verily I say unto you, They have their reward.

MATTHEW 6:5

12.

Then shall they call upon me, but I will not
answer; they shall seek me early, but they shall
not find me: For that they hated knowledge, and
did not choose the fear of the LORD: They would
none of my counsel: they despised all my reproof.
Therefore shall they eat of the fruit of their own
way, and be filled with their own devices.

PROVERBS 1:28–31

13.

But when ye pray, use not vain repetitions, as the heathen do: for they think that they shall be heard for their much speaking. Be not ye therefore like unto them: for your Father knoweth what things ye have need of, before ye ask him.

Matthew 6:7–8

14.

Ye ask, and receive not, because ye ask amiss, that ye may consume it upon your lusts.

James 4:3

15.

But let him ask in faith, nothing wavering. For he that wavereth is like a wave of the sea driven with the wind and tossed. For let not that man think that he shall receive any thing of the Lord. A double minded man is unstable in all his ways.

James 1:6-8

16.

If I regard iniquity in my heart,
the Lord will not hear me.

PSALM 66:18

17.

Because I have called, and ye refused; I have
stretched out my hand, and no man regarded;
But ye have set at nought all my counsel, and
would none of my reproof: I also will laugh at
your calamity; I will mock when your fear cometh.

PROVERBS 1:24–26

18.

He that turneth away his ear from hearing the
law, even his prayer shall be abomination.

PROVERBS 28:9

19.

Whoso stoppeth his ears at the cry of the poor,
he also shall cry himself, but shall not be heard.

PROVERBS 21:13

20.

And the publican, standing afar off, would not lift
up so much as his eyes unto heaven, but smote
upon his breast, saying, God be merciful to me
a sinner. I tell you, this man went down to his
house justified rather than the other: for every
one that exalteth himself shall be abased; and he
that humbleth himself shall be exalted.

LUKE 18:13–14

WHY SHOULD YOU PRAY?

Heavenly Father, I come to You in prayer for so many reasons. Sometimes I am seeking Your forgiveness. Other times I am lost, and I need You to grant me wisdom in a decision I must make. I bow before You in thanksgiving. I cry out to You for relief from distress or illness. You are a good God. You meet me where I am. Remind me that I am to pray at all times—and in every circumstance. Challenge me, Lord, and guide me to pray in ways I never knew possible. I know that prayer changes things. In Jesus' name I pray, amen.

21.

And I say unto you, Ask, and it shall be given you; seek, and ye shall find; knock, and it shall be opened unto you. For every one that asketh receiveth; and he that seeketh findeth; and to him that knocketh it shall be opened.

LUKE 11:9–10

22.

Continue in prayer, and watch in the same with thanksgiving.

COLOSSIANS 4:2

23.

What shall I render unto the LORD for all his benefits toward me? . . . I will offer to thee the sacrifice of thanksgiving, and will call upon the name of the LORD.

PSALM 116:12, 17

24.

And he came out, and went, as he was wont, to the mount of Olives; and his disciples also followed him. And when he was at the place, he said unto them, Pray that ye enter not into temptation.

LUKE 22:39–40

25.

I acknowledge my sin unto thee, and mine iniquity have I not hid. I said, I will confess my transgressions unto the LORD; and thou forgavest the iniquity of my sin. Selah. For this shall every one that is godly pray unto thee in a time when thou mayest be found: surely in the floods of great waters they shall not come nigh unto him.

PSALM 32:5–6

26.

Speaking to yourselves in psalms and hymns
and spiritual songs, singing and making
melody in your heart to the Lord; Giving
thanks always for all things unto God and the
Father in the name of our Lord Jesus Christ.

EPHESIANS 5:19–20

27.

For every creature of God is good, and nothing
to be refused, if it be received with thanksgiving:
For it is sanctified by the word of God and prayer.

1 TIMOTHY 4:4–5

28.

Hear me when I call, O God of my righteousness:
thou hast enlarged me when I was in distress;
have mercy upon me, and hear my prayer.

PSALM 4:1

29.

For this cause I bow my knees unto the Father of our Lord Jesus Christ, Of whom the whole family in heaven and earth is named, That he would grant you, according to the riches of his glory, to be strengthened with might by his Spirit in the inner man; That Christ may dwell in your hearts by faith; that ye, being rooted and grounded in love, May be able to comprehend with all saints what is the breadth, and length, and depth, and height; And to know the love of Christ, which passeth knowledge, that ye might be filled with all the fulness of God.

EPHESIANS 3:14–19

30.

Submit yourselves therefore to God. Resist the devil, and he will flee from you. Draw nigh to God, and he will draw nigh to you. Cleanse your hands, ye sinners; and purify your hearts, ye double minded. Be afflicted, and mourn, and weep: let your laughter be turned to mourning, and your joy to heaviness. Humble yourselves in the sight of the Lord, and he shall lift you up.

JAMES 4:7–10

WHEN SHOULD
YOU PRAY?

*Lord, I come to You in the morning, afternoon, and
evening. I seek Your face before I even start my day.
Remind me that I am called to pray without ceasing,
making prayer a constant in my life—just like breathing.
Father, I ask that You would help me not to view prayer
as a ritual or a duty, but that it might truly be an
ongoing conversation with my Abba Father, my Creator,
my Daddy. In Jesus' name I pray, amen.*

31.

And take the helmet of salvation, and the
sword of the Spirit, which is the word of God:
Praying always with all prayer and supplication
in the Spirit, and watching thereunto with all
perseverance and supplication for all saints.

EPHESIANS 6:17–18

32.

As for me, I will call upon God; and the
LORD shall save me. Evening, and morning,
and at noon, will I pray, and cry aloud:
and he shall hear my voice.

PSALM 55:16–17

33.

For if I by grace be a partaker, why am I evil
spoken of for that for which I give thanks?
Whether therefore ye eat, or drink, or whatsoever
ye do, do all to the glory of God.

1 CORINTHIANS 10:30–31

34.

And he commanded the people to sit down
on the ground: and he took the seven loaves,
and gave thanks, and brake, and gave to his
disciples to set before them; and they did
set them before the people.

MARK 8:6

35.

Stand in awe, and sin not: commune with
your own heart upon your bed, and be still.

PSALM 4:4

36.

And when they had prayed, the place was shaken
where they were assembled together; and they
were all filled with the Holy Ghost, and they
spake the word of God with boldness.

ACTS 4:31

37.

Confess your faults one to another, and pray one
for another, that ye may be healed. The effectual
fervent prayer of a righteous man availeth much.

JAMES 5:16

38.

And he spake a parable unto them to this end,
that men ought always to pray, and not to faint.

LUKE 18:1

39.

Pray without ceasing.

1 THESSALONIANS 5:17

40.

O lord God of my salvation, I have
cried day and night before thee.

PSALM 88:1

TYPES OF PRAYER

Lord, as I learn more about prayer, I realize it is so much more than bombarding You with a list of wants. There are as many types of prayers as there are types of conversations. And prayer really is a conversation with You, Father. May I first and foremost praise Your holy name. When I see a need, may I bring it before Your throne. May I feel confident to lay my own burdens and needs at Your feet. May I always be mindful to confess my sins. Lord, I thank You that I can come before You in many types of prayer. I ask all of this in Jesus' name, amen.

41.

Again I say unto you, That if two of you
shall agree on earth as touching any thing
that they shall ask, it shall be done for
them of my Father which is in heaven.

MATTHEW 18:19

42.

Therefore I say unto you, What things
soever ye desire, when ye pray, believe that
ye receive them, and ye shall have them.

MARK 11:24

43.

Wherefore I also, after I heard of your faith in the Lord Jesus, and love unto all the saints, Cease not to give thanks for you, making mention of you in my prayers; That the God of our Lord Jesus Christ, the Father of glory, may give unto you the spirit of wisdom and revelation in the knowledge of him: The eyes of your understanding being enlightened; that ye may know what is the hope of his calling, and what the riches of the glory of his inheritance in the saints.

EPHESIANS 1:15–18

44.

Praise ye the LORD. I will praise the LORD with my whole heart, in the assembly of the upright, and in the congregation. The works of the LORD are great, sought out of all them that have pleasure therein. His work is honourable and glorious: and his righteousness endureth for ever. He hath made his wonderful works to be remembered: the LORD is gracious and full of compassion.

PSALM 111:1–4

45.

If we confess our sins, he is faithful and
just to forgive us our sins, and to cleanse
us from all unrighteousness.

1 John 1:9

46.

Is any among you afflicted? let him pray. Is any
merry? let him sing psalms. Is any sick among
you? let him call for the elders of the church;
and let them pray over him, anointing him with
oil in the name of the Lord: And the prayer of
faith shall save the sick, and the Lord shall
raise him up; and if he have committed sins,
they shall be forgiven him.

James 5:13–15

47.

Bless the Lord, O my soul: and all that is
within me, bless his holy name. Bless the Lord,
O my soul, and forget not all his benefits.

Psalm 103:1–2

48.

For we wrestle not against flesh and blood,
but against principalities, against powers,
against the rulers of the darkness of this world,
against spiritual wickedness in high places.

EPHESIANS 6:12

49.

And I say unto you, Ask, and it shall be
given you; seek, and ye shall find; knock,
and it shall be opened unto you.

LUKE 11:9

50.

And he went a little farther, and fell on his
face, and prayed, saying, O my Father, if it
be possible, let this cup pass from me:
nevertheless not as I will, but as thou wilt.

MATTHEW 26:39

PRAYERS OF THE BIBLE

Lord, the prayers of the Bible inspire me. I can almost see Hannah's tears. . .feel Moses' fervent pleading with You. Make me a prayer warrior like the ancient heroes and heroines of the faith. The spiritual discipline in their lives regularly led them to Your throne. Give me the desire and the endurance to have such discipline. I want to be a person of prayer, because prayer changes things. In Jesus' name I pray, amen.

51.

And Jabez called on the God of Israel, saying, Oh that thou wouldest bless me indeed, and enlarge my coast, and that thine hand might be with me, and that thou wouldest keep me from evil, that it may not grieve me! And God granted him that which he requested.

1 Chronicles 4:10

52.

Then said Jesus, Father, forgive them; for they know not what they do.

Luke 23:34

53.

And said, I cried by reason of mine affliction unto the LORD, and he heard me; out of the belly of hell cried I, and thou heardest my voice. For thou hadst cast me into the deep, in the midst of the seas; and the floods compassed me about: all thy billows and thy waves passed over me.

JONAH 2:2–3

54.

Lord, how are they increased that trouble me! many are they that rise up against me. Many there be which say of my soul, There is no help for him in God. Selah. But thou, O LORD, art a shield for me; my glory, and the lifter up of mine head. I cried unto the LORD with my voice, and he heard me out of his holy hill.

PSALM 3:1–4

55.

Now therefore, O LORD our God, I beseech thee, save thou us out of his hand, that all the kingdoms of the earth may know that thou art the LORD God, even thou only.

2 KINGS 19:19

56.

And Hannah prayed, and said, My heart
rejoiceth in the Lord, mine horn is exalted in the
Lord: my mouth is enlarged over mine enemies;
because I rejoice in thy salvation. There is none
holy as the Lord: for there is none beside thee:
neither is there any rock like our God.

1 Samuel 2:1–2

57.

O lord, thou hast searched me, and known me.
Thou knowest my downsitting and mine up-
rising, thou understandest my thought afar off.
Thou compassest my path and my lying down,
and art acquainted with all my ways. For there is
not a word in my tongue, but, lo, O Lord, thou
knowest it altogether. Thou hast beset me behind
and before, and laid thine hand upon me.

Psalm 139:1–5

58.

If it be so, our God whom we serve is able
to deliver us from the burning fiery furnace,
and he will deliver us out of thine hand, O king.
But if not, be it known unto thee, O king, that
we will not serve thy gods, nor worship the
golden image which thou hast set up.

Daniel 3:17–18

59.

I will praise thee, O LORD, with my whole heart; I will shew forth all thy marvellous works. I will be glad and rejoice in thee: I will sing praise to thy name, O thou most High.

PSALM 9:1–2

60.

And Moses besought the LORD his God, and said, LORD, why doth thy wrath wax hot against thy people, which thou hast brought forth out of the land of Egypt with great power, and with a mighty hand? Wherefore should the Egyptians speak, and say, For mischief did he bring them out, to slay them in the mountains, and to consume them from the face of the earth? Turn from thy fierce wrath, and repent of this evil against thy people. Remember Abraham, Isaac, and Israel, thy servants, to whom thou swarest by thine own self, and saidst unto them, I will multiply your seed as the stars of heaven, and all this land that I have spoken of will I give unto your seed, and they shall inherit it for ever. And the LORD repented of the evil which he thought to do unto his people.

EXODUS 32:11–14

THE LORD'S PRAYER

Lord Jesus, thank You for giving believers a model for prayer. When Your disciples asked You to teach them to pray, You were ready with an answer. The Lord's Prayer reminds me to address God as my holy Father. I am to acknowledge that Your will is not my own. I can ask You for what I need, confess my sins, and request Your protection from Satan as he tempts me to sin. May I always remember to pray in such a manner, even if I use my own words. Hear my heart now as I pray the Lord's Prayer. Amen.

61.

After this manner therefore pray ye: Our Father which art in heaven, Hallowed be thy name. Thy kingdom come, Thy will be done in earth, as it is in heaven. Give us this day our daily bread. And forgive us our debts, as we forgive our debtors. And lead us not into temptation, but deliver us from evil: For thine is the kingdom, and the power, and the glory, for ever. Amen.

Matthew 6:9–13

62.

And he said unto them, When ye pray, say, Our
Father which art in heaven, Hallowed be thy
name. Thy kingdom come. Thy will be done, as
in heaven, so in earth. Give us day by day our
daily bread. And forgive us our sins; for we also
forgive every one that is indebted to us. And lead
us not into temptation; but deliver us from evil.

Luke 11:2–4

63.

And it came to pass, that, as he was praying
in a certain place, when he ceased, one of his
disciples said unto him, Lord, teach us to
pray, as John also taught his disciples.

Luke 11:1

64.

Therefore take no thought, saying, What shall
we eat? or, What shall we drink? or, Wherewithal
shall we be clothed? (For after all these things
do the Gentiles seek:) for your heavenly Father
knoweth that ye have need of all these things.

Matthew 6:31–32

65.

For if ye forgive men their trespasses,
your heavenly Father will also forgive you:
But if ye forgive not men their trespasses,
neither will your Father forgive your trespasses.

Matthew 6:14–15

66.

If we confess our sins, he is faithful
and just to forgive us our sins, and to
cleanse us from all unrighteousness.

1 John 1:9

67.

Or what man is there of you, whom if his son
ask bread, will he give him a stone? Or if he
ask a fish, will he give him a serpent? If ye then,
being evil, know how to give good gifts unto your
children, how much more shall your Father which
is in heaven give good things to them that ask him?

Matthew 7:9–11

68.

For this cause I bow my knees unto the Father
of our Lord Jesus Christ, Of whom the whole
family in heaven and earth is named.

EPHESIANS 3:14–15

69.

In that hour Jesus rejoiced in spirit, and said, I
thank thee, O Father, Lord of heaven and earth,
that thou hast hid these things from the wise and
prudent, and hast revealed them unto babes: even
so, Father; for so it seemed good in thy sight.

LUKE 10:21

70.

And when ye stand praying, forgive, if ye have
ought against any: that your Father also which is
in heaven may forgive you your trespasses.

MARK 11:25

GOD ANSWERS PRAYERS

Heavenly Father, You are faithful to answer the prayers of Your children. Please give me the confidence to come before You in prayer with a thankful heart, asking You to bless me. Remind me that Your answer may not always be what I want, but You are my Father and You always have my best interests at heart. I am encouraged by the times I can trace Your hand in my life and see where You answered my prayers. Please help me to be disciplined in my prayer life so I can see You at work! In Jesus' name, amen.

71.
And this is the confidence that we have in him,
that, if we ask any thing according to his will,
he heareth us: And if we know that he hear us,
whatsoever we ask, we know that we have
the petitions that we desired of him.
1 JOHN 5:14–15

72.
And it shall come to pass, that before
they call, I will answer; and while
they are yet speaking, I will hear.
ISAIAH 65:24

73.

There hath no temptation taken you but such as is common to man: but God is faithful, who will not suffer you to be tempted above that ye are able; but will with the temptation also make a way to escape, that ye may be able to bear it.

1 Corinthians 10:13

74.

Therefore I will look unto the Lord; I will wait for the God of my salvation: my God will hear me.

Micah 7:7

75.

And the prayer of faith shall save the sick, and the Lord shall raise him up; and if he have committed sins, they shall be forgiven him. Confess your faults one to another, and pray one for another, that ye may be healed. The effectual fervent prayer of a righteous man availeth much.

James 5:15–16

76.

And whatsoever ye shall ask in my name, that
will I do, that the Father may be glorified in the
Son. If ye shall ask any thing in my name, I will
do it. If ye love me, keep my commandments.

JOHN 14:13–15

77.

Let us therefore come boldly unto the
throne of grace, that we may obtain mercy,
and find grace to help in time of need.

HEBREWS 4:16

78.

If my people, which are called by my name,
shall humble themselves, and pray, and seek
my face, and turn from their wicked ways;
then will I hear from heaven, and will forgive
their sin, and will heal their land. Now mine
eyes shall be open, and mine ears attent unto
the prayer that is made in this place.

2 CHRONICLES 7:14–15

79.

Thus saith the LORD the maker thereof,
the LORD that formed it, to establish it;
the LORD is his name; Call unto me, and I
will answer thee, and show thee great and
mighty things, which thou knowest not.

JEREMIAH 33:2–3

80.

But without faith it is impossible to please
him: for he that cometh to God must believe
that he is, and that he is a rewarder of
them that diligently seek him.

HEBREWS 11:6

PRAYING FOR PEACE

God, help me to discover true peace. I know it is only available through Your Son, Jesus. Many people and programs offer peace in this world, but none satisfies fully like Your Son. I pray that peace will be at the center of my heart and my home all the days of my life. When I see a person who walks closely with You, his or her life is always marked by an undeniable peace. That is what I want. Please show me the way. Today, begin to fill me with the peace that passes all understanding. Thank You, Lord. Amen.

81.
And the peace of God, which passeth
all understanding, shall keep your hearts
and minds through Christ Jesus.

PHILIPPIANS 4:7

———•◦•———

82.
Now the God of hope fill you with all joy and
peace in believing, that ye may abound in hope,
through the power of the Holy Ghost.

ROMANS 15:13

83.

For they that are after the flesh do mind
the things of the flesh; but they that are
after the Spirit the things of the Spirit.
For to be carnally minded is death; but to
be spiritually minded is life and peace.

ROMANS 8:5–6

84.

Great peace have they which love thy law:
and nothing shall offend them.

PSALM 119:165

85.

Be careful for nothing; but in every thing
by prayer and supplication with thanksgiving
let your requests be made known unto God.

PHILIPPIANS 4:6

86.

My son, let not them depart from thine eyes:
keep sound wisdom and discretion: So shall
they be life unto thy soul, and grace to thy neck.
Then shalt thou walk in thy way safely, and thy
foot shall not stumble. When thou liest down,
thou shalt not be afraid: yea, thou shalt lie
down, and thy sleep shall be sweet.

PROVERBS 3:21–24

87.

Come unto me, all ye that labour and
are heavy laden, and I will give you rest.

MATTHEW 11:28

88.

Peace I leave with you, my peace I give unto you:
not as the world giveth, give I unto you. Let not
your heart be troubled, neither let it be afraid.

JOHN 14:27

89.

I will both lay me down in peace, and sleep:
for thou, Lord, only makest me dwell in safety.

Psalm 4:8

90.

Wherefore take unto you the whole armour
of God, that ye may be able to withstand in
the evil day, and having done all, to stand.
Stand therefore, having your loins girt about
with truth, and having on the breastplate of
righteousness; And your feet shod with the
preparation of the gospel of peace.

Ephesians 6:13–15

PRAYING FOR DIRECTION

*God, thank You for the privilege to be able to come to
You in prayer. You tell me to seek You with my whole
heart and to come before Your throne with confidence.
I am Your child, made righteous only through Christ
Jesus. May I never forget where my help comes from—
my help comes from the Lord, the Maker of heaven
and earth. I humbly ask for wisdom, discernment,
and guidance. In the name of Jesus I pray, amen.*

91.

Woe unto him that saith to the wood, Awake;
to the dumb stone, Arise, it shall teach! Behold,
it is laid over with gold and silver, and there
is no breath at all in the midst of it.

HABAKKUK 2:19

92.

And thine ears shall hear a word behind
thee, saying, This is the way, walk ye
in it, when ye turn to the right hand,
and when ye turn to the left.

ISAIAH 30:21

93.

And the LORD shall guide thee continually, and
satisfy thy soul in drought, and make fat thy
bones: and thou shalt be like a watered garden,
and like a spring of water, whose waters fail not.

ISAIAH 58:11

94.

But the Comforter, which is the Holy Ghost,
whom the Father will send in my name, he shall
teach you all things, and bring all things to your
remembrance, whatsoever I have said unto you.

JOHN 14:26

95.

Regard not them that have familiar spirits,
neither seek after wizards, to be defiled
by them: I am the LORD your God.

LEVITICUS 19:31

96.

A man's heart deviseth his way:
but the LORD directeth his steps.

PROVERBS 16:9

97.

I will instruct thee and teach thee
in the way which thou shalt go:
I will guide thee with mine eye.

PSALM 32:8

98.

The steps of a good man are ordered by the
LORD: and he delighteth in his way. Though
he fall, he shall not be utterly cast down:
for the LORD upholdeth him with his hand.

PSALM 37:23–24

99.
Thy word is a lamp unto my feet,
and a light unto my path.
PSALM 119:105

———————— ••• ————————

100.
Trust in the LORD with all thine heart; and
lean not unto thine own understanding.
In all thy ways acknowledge him,
and he shall direct thy paths.
PROVERBS 3:5–6

PRAYING FOR ASSURANCE OF SALVATION

Lord, I am so thankful that I never have doubt. . . . I don't have to wonder. I am assured of my salvation through Jesus Christ. Whenever I feel far away from You, I know that I am the one who has moved. You are steadfast through the ages—the same yesterday, today, and forever. Your promises are sure. I know that my salvation is not based on anything I do, but on Your grace and through my faith in Christ alone. Thank You for this blessed assurance that is mine. In Jesus' name I pray, amen.

101.

Therefore being justified by faith, we have peace with God through our Lord Jesus Christ.

ROMANS 5:1

———— •‣•‣• ————

102.

These things have I written unto you that believe on the name of the Son of God; that ye may know that ye have eternal life, and that ye may believe on the name of the Son of God.

1 JOHN 5:13

103.

Therefore also now, saith the LORD, turn ye even to me with all your heart, and with fasting, and with weeping, and with mourning: And rend your heart, and not your garments, and turn unto the LORD your God: for he is gracious and merciful, slow to anger, and of great kindness, and repenteth him of the evil.

JOEL 2:12–13

104.

For God so loved the world, that he gave his only begotten Son, that whosoever believeth in him should not perish, but have everlasting life.

JOHN 3:16

105.

In whom ye also trusted, after that ye heard the word of truth, the gospel of your salvation: in whom also after that ye believed, ye were sealed with that holy Spirit of promise, Which is the earnest of our inheritance until the redemption of the purchased possession, unto the praise of his glory.

EPHESIANS 1:13–14

106.

The Lord is merciful and gracious, slow to anger, and plenteous in mercy. He will not always chide: neither will he keep his anger for ever. He hath not dealt with us after our sins; nor rewarded us according to our iniquities. For as the heaven is high above the earth, so great is his mercy toward them that fear him. As far as the east is from the west, so far hath he removed our transgressions from us.

Psalm 103:8–12

107.

All that the Father giveth me shall come to me; and him that cometh to me I will in no wise cast out.

John 6:37

108.

For by grace are ye saved through faith; and that not of yourselves: it is the gift of God: Not of works, lest any man should boast.

Ephesians 2:8–9

109.

Being confident of this very thing, that he
which hath begun a good work in you will
perform it until the day of Jesus Christ.

PHILIPPIANS 1:6

———————●•●———————

110.

And we desire that every one of you do
shew the same diligence to the full
assurance of hope unto the end.

HEBREWS 6:11

PRAYING FOR WISDOM

*Lord, there are so many voices competing for my ear
in this world today. May I hear Your voice clearly
above them all. You are the Good Shepherd, and You
know Your sheep. . .and Your sheep know Your voice.
I long for wisdom. Your Word assures me that if I seek
wisdom, You will give it to me. I have personally known
some of the wisest people, and they are not powerful
or important in worldly terms. But they are humble
servants who seek You with their whole heart. Make me
such a person. I ask in Jesus' name, amen.*

111.

If any of you lack wisdom, let him ask of
God, that giveth to all men liberally, and
upbraideth not; and it shall be given him.

JAMES 1:5

112.

For wisdom is better than rubies; and all
the things that may be desired are not to be
compared to it. I wisdom dwell with prudence,
and find out knowledge of witty inventions.

PROVERBS 8:11–12

113.

Cease not to give thanks for you, making mention of you in my prayers; That the God of our Lord Jesus Christ, the Father of glory, may give unto you the spirit of wisdom and revelation in the knowledge of him.

EPHESIANS 1:16–17

114.

For I will give you a mouth and wisdom, which all your adversaries shall not be able to gainsay nor resist.

LUKE 21:15

115.

O the depth of the riches both of the wisdom and knowledge of God! how unsearchable are his judgments, and his ways past finding out!

ROMANS 11:33

116.

Happy is the man that findeth wisdom,
and the man that getteth understanding.

PROVERBS 3:13

117.

Which things also we speak, not in the
words which man's wisdom teacheth,
but which the Holy Ghost teacheth;
comparing spiritual things with spiritual.

1 CORINTHIANS 2:13

118.

But the wisdom that is from above is first
pure, then peaceable, gentle, and easy to be
intreated, full of mercy and good fruits,
without partiality, and without hypocrisy.

JAMES 3:17

119.

I applied mine heart to know, and to search,
and to seek out wisdom, and the reason of
things, and to know the wickedness of folly,
even of foolishness and madness.

ECCLESIASTES 7:25

120.

See then that ye walk circumspectly, not as fools,
but as wise, Redeeming the time, because the
days are evil. Wherefore be ye not unwise,
but understanding what the will of the Lord is.

EPHESIANS 5:15–17

PRAYING FOR MISSIONARIES

Heavenly Father, I know we are called to share the Gospel with others. Some people do this in their own homes and places of work. Others are called to full-time ministry as missionaries. I lift up the Christian missionaries all around the world. I ask that You would strengthen them and remind them of Your calling and Your promise to provide for them. I pray they would have opportunities to share Your Good News and that many will come to know You as a result. As I pray for missionaries, I am challenged to be ministry-minded in my own daily life. Use me to spread Your Word, just as you use career missionaries. Amen.

121.
Go ye therefore, and teach all nations,
baptizing them in the name of the Father,
and of the Son, and of the Holy Ghost: Teaching
them to observe all things whatsoever I have
commanded you: and, lo, I am with you always,
even unto the end of the world. Amen.
MATTHEW 28:19–20

122.

For so hath the Lord commanded us, saying,
I have set thee to be a light of the Gentiles,
that thou shouldest be for salvation
unto the ends of the earth.

ACTS 13:47

123.

For whosoever shall call upon the name
of the Lord shall be saved. How then shall
they call on him in whom they have not
believed? and how shall they believe in him
of whom they have not heard? and how
shall they hear without a preacher?

ROMANS 10:13–14

124.

Declare his glory among the heathen;
his marvellous works among all nations.

1 CHRONICLES 16:24

125.

So, as much as in me is, I am ready to preach
the gospel to you that are at Rome also. For I am
not ashamed of the gospel of Christ: for it is the
power of God unto salvation to every one that
believeth; to the Jew first, and also to the Greek.

ROMANS 1:15–16

126.

Therefore, my beloved brethren, be ye stedfast,
unmoveable, always abounding in the work
of the Lord, forasmuch as ye know that your
labour is not in vain in the Lord.

1 CORINTHIANS 15:58

127.

Not slothful in business; fervent in spirit;
serving the Lord; Rejoicing in hope; patient
in tribulation; continuing instant in prayer.

ROMANS 12:11–12

128.

But my God shall supply all your need
according to his riches in glory by Christ
Jesus. Now unto God and our Father
be glory for ever and ever. Amen.

PHILIPPIANS 4:19–20

129.

For even hereunto were ye called: because
Christ also suffered for us, leaving us an example,
that ye should follow his steps: Who did no
sin, neither was guile found in his mouth: Who,
when he was reviled, reviled not again; when he
suffered, he threatened not; but committed
himself to him that judgeth righteously.

1 PETER 2:21–23

130.

Withal praying also for us, that God would open
unto us a door of utterance, to speak the mystery
of Christ, for which I am also in bonds.

COLOSSIANS 4:3

INTERCESSORY PRAYER

Heavenly Father, I am honored to come before You in prayer for my brothers and sisters. May I never reduce prayer to a checklist or a time to pour out my own woes at Your feet, Lord. Bring to mind those whom You would have me pray for, and make me disciplined in following through. Prayer allows me a front-row seat as I watch You at work in the lives of others. Thank You for the privilege of intercessory prayer. In Jesus' name, amen.

131.

Praying always with all prayer and supplication in the Spirit, and watching thereunto with all perseverance and supplication for all saints.

EPHESIANS 6:18

132.

And in that day ye shall ask me nothing. Verily, verily, I say unto you, Whatsoever ye shall ask the Father in my name, he will give it you. Hitherto have ye asked nothing in my name: ask, and ye shall receive, that your joy may be full.

JOHN 16:23–24

133.

Ye have heard that it hath been said, Thou shalt
love thy neighbour, and hate thine enemy. But
I say unto you, Love your enemies, bless them
that curse you, do good to them that hate you,
and pray for them which despitefully use you,
and persecute you; That ye may be the children
of your Father which is in heaven: for he maketh
his sun to rise on the evil and on the good, and
sendeth rain on the just and on the unjust.

MATTHEW 5:43–45

134.

Is any sick among you? let him call for the
elders of the church; and let them pray over him,
anointing him with oil in the name of the Lord:
And the prayer of faith shall save the sick, and the
Lord shall raise him up; and if he have committed
sins, they shall be forgiven him. Confess your
faults one to another, and pray one for another,
that ye may be healed. The effectual fervent
prayer of a righteous man availeth much.

JAMES 5:14–16

135.

And he gave some, apostles; and some,
prophets; and some, evangelists; and some,
pastors and teachers; For the perfecting of
the saints, for the work of the ministry,
for the edifying of the body of Christ.

Ephesians 4:11–12

136.

I exhort therefore, that, first of all,
supplications, prayers, intercessions,
and giving of thanks, be made for all men.

1 Timothy 2:1

137.

And he saw that there was no man, and
wondered that there was no intercessor:
therefore his arm brought salvation unto him;
and his righteousness, it sustained him.

Isaiah 59:16

138.

For this cause I bow my knees unto the Father
of our Lord Jesus Christ, Of whom the whole
family in heaven and earth is named, That he
would grant you, according to the riches of his
glory, to be strengthened with might by his
Spirit in the inner man; That Christ may
dwell in your hearts by faith.

EPHESIANS 3:14–17

139.

For this cause we also, since the day we heard it,
do not cease to pray for you, and to desire that
ye might be filled with the knowledge of his will
in all wisdom and spiritual understanding.

COLOSSIANS 1:9

140.

And this I pray, that your love may abound
yet more and more in knowledge and in all
judgment; That ye may approve things that
are excellent; that ye may be sincere and
without offence till the day of Christ.

PHILIPPIANS 1:9–10

THE POWER OF PRAYER

Dear God, You are mighty and sovereign. You spoke, and there was light. You created the world, and You are sovereign over it. In fact, the very breath in my lungs is Yours! And yet, You commune with me. You hear my prayers. You use me and bless me and guide me. Thank You for the power of prayer. The prayers of the saints in the Bible really shook things up at times! May I be a prayer warrior who is on my knees for others and for myself. May I be an eyewitness to the great power found in prayer to You, the Living God. Amen.

141.

Confess your faults one to another, and pray one for another, that ye may be healed. The effectual fervent prayer of a righteous man availeth much. Elias was a man subject to like passions as we are, and he prayed earnestly that it might not rain: and it rained not on the earth by the space of three years and six months. And he prayed again, and the heaven gave rain, and the earth brought forth her fruit.

JAMES 5:16–18

142.

And whatsoever we ask, we receive of him,
because we keep his commandments, and do
those things that are pleasing in his sight.

1 John 3:22

143.

If any of you lack wisdom, let him ask of
God, that giveth to all men liberally, and
upbraideth not; and it shall be given him.

James 1:5

144.

For we have not an high priest which cannot
be touched with the feeling of our infirmities;
but was in all points tempted like as we are, yet
without sin. Let us therefore come boldly unto
the throne of grace, that we may obtain mercy,
and find grace to help in time of need.

Hebrews 4:15–16

145.

And when he was come into the house,
his disciples asked him privately, Why could
not we cast him out? And he said unto them,
This kind can come forth by nothing,
but by prayer and fasting.

MARK 9:28–29

146.

Then they cry unto the LORD in their
trouble, and he bringeth them out of
their distresses. He maketh the storm
a calm, so that the waves thereof are still.

PSALM 107:28–29

147.

Ask, and it shall be given you; seek, and ye shall
find; knock, and it shall be opened unto you.

MATTHEW 7:7

148.

But let him ask in faith, nothing wavering.
For he that wavereth is like a wave of the
sea driven with the wind and tossed.

James 1:6

149.

Jesus answered and said unto them, Verily I say
unto you, If ye have faith, and doubt not, ye
shall not only do this which is done to the fig
tree, but also if ye shall say unto this mountain,
Be thou removed, and be thou cast into the sea;
it shall be done. And all things, whatsoever ye
shall ask in prayer, believing, ye shall receive.

Matthew 21:21–22

150.

Then shall ye call upon me, and ye shall go and
pray unto me, and I will hearken unto you.

Jeremiah 29:12

PRAYING AS
JESUS PRAYED

*Jesus, as I read Your Word, I learn how You prayed
when You were here on earth. You prayed often. You
prayed in nature. You prayed for Yourself and for
others. You prayed earnestly. . .sometimes all alone and
sometimes in the company of others. You prayed big
prayers, believing God for great things; and You also
prayed for children, whom some considered insignificant
in Your day. Lord Jesus, may I learn from the way You
prayed. May I become a prayer warrior whose prayers
avail much. Amen.*

151.

And it came to pass in those days,
that he went out into a mountain to pray,
and continued all night in prayer to God.

LUKE 6:12

152.

And he went a little farther, and fell on his
face, and prayed, saying, O my Father,
if it be possible, let this cup pass from me:
nevertheless not as I will, but as thou wilt.

MATTHEW 26:39

153.

Then they took away the stone from the place where the dead was laid. And Jesus lifted up his eyes, and said, Father, I thank thee that thou hast heard me. And I knew that thou hearest me always: but because of the people which stand by I said it, that they may believe that thou hast sent me. And when he thus had spoken, he cried with a loud voice, Lazarus, come forth. And he that was dead came forth, bound hand and foot with graveclothes: and his face was bound about with a napkin. Jesus saith unto them, Loose him, and let him go.

JOHN 11:41–44

154.

These words spake Jesus, and lifted up his eyes to heaven, and said, Father, the hour is come; glorify thy Son, that thy Son also may glorify thee: As thou hast given him power over all flesh, that he should give eternal life to as many as thou hast given him. And this is life eternal, that they might know thee the only true God, and Jesus Christ, whom thou hast sent.

JOHN 17:1–3

155.

For we have not an high priest which
cannot be touched with the feeling of our
infirmities; but was in all points tempted
like as we are, yet without sin.

HEBREWS 4:15

156.

I pray for them: I pray not for the world,
but for them which thou hast given me;
for they are thine. And all mine are thine,
and thine are mine; and I am glorified in them.

JOHN 17:9–10

157.

And it came to pass about an eight days after
these sayings, he took Peter and John and James,
and went up into a mountain to pray. And as
he prayed, the fashion of his countenance was
altered, and his raiment was white and glistering.

LUKE 9:28–29

158.

Then said Jesus, Father, forgive them;
for they know not what they do.
And they parted his raiment, and cast lots.

LUKE 23:34

159.

But so much the more went there a fame
abroad of him: and great multitudes came
together to hear, and to be healed by him of
their infirmities. And he withdrew himself
into the wilderness, and prayed.

LUKE 5:15–16

160.

Then were there brought unto him little
children, that he should put his hands on them,
and pray: and the disciples rebuked them.
But Jesus said, Suffer little children, and forbid
them not, to come unto me: for of such is the
kingdom of heaven. And he laid his hands
on them, and departed thence.

MATTHEW 19:13–15

PRAYING WHEN
WORRIED

Father, You tell me not to worry and to let each day take care of itself. You remind me not to borrow trouble. And yet I find it so difficult! There are so many hardships and disappointments in this life. My family and friends have so many needs. I worry about them right along with my own issues. Help me to lay down my worries as I come to You in prayer. When I cast my cares at Your throne of grace, my troubles grow smaller as Your love encompasses me. Amen.

161.
Come unto me, all ye that labour and are heavy laden, and I will give you rest. Take my yoke upon you, and learn of me; for I am meek and lowly in heart: and ye shall find rest unto your souls. For my yoke is easy, and my burden is light.

MATTHEW 11:28–30

162.
Cast thy burden upon the LORD,
and he shall sustain thee: he shall never
suffer the righteous to be moved.

PSALM 55:22

163.

Yea, though I walk through the valley of the
shadow of death, I will fear no evil: for thou art
with me; thy rod and thy staff they comfort me.

PSALM 23:4

164.

Therefore I say unto you, Take no thought
for your life, what ye shall eat, or what ye shall
drink; nor yet for your body, what ye shall put
on. Is not the life more than meat, and the body
than raiment? Behold the fowls of the air: for they
sow not, neither do they reap, nor gather into
barns; yet your heavenly Father feedeth them.
Are ye not much better than they?

MATTHEW 6:25–26

165.

And seek not ye what ye shall eat, or what ye
shall drink, neither be ye of doubtful mind.
For all these things do the nations of the
world seek after: and your Father knoweth
that ye have need of these things.

LUKE 12:29–30

166.

Heaviness in the heart of man maketh it stoop:
but a good word maketh it glad.

PROVERBS 12:25

167.

Let your conversation be without covetousness;
and be content with such things as ye have: for he
hath said, I will never leave thee, nor forsake thee.
So that we may boldly say, The Lord is my helper,
and I will not fear what man shall do unto me.

HEBREWS 13:5–6

168.

The LORD also will be a refuge for the oppressed,
a refuge in times of trouble.

PSALM 9:9

169.

The righteous cry, and the LORD heareth,
and delivereth them out of all their troubles.
The LORD is nigh unto them that are of a broken
heart; and saveth such as be of a contrite spirit.
Many are the afflictions of the righteous: but
the LORD delivereth him out of them all.

PSALM 34:17–19

170.

For thou hast been a shelter for me,
and a strong tower from the enemy.

PSALM 61:3

PRAYING IN THE SPIRIT

*Dear Lord, how wonderful that, as a believer in Christ,
I have the Holy Spirit living within me! I can pray in
the power of the Spirit, by the leading of the Spirit, and
according to Your will. Please teach me how to do this
more and more each day. What a blessing to know that
the Spirit intercedes for me when I don't know what to
pray! In Jesus' name, and through the power of the Holy
Spirit, I pray, amen.*

171.

Likewise the Spirit also helpeth our infirmities:
for we know not what we should pray for as we
ought: but the Spirit itself maketh intercession
for us with groanings which cannot be uttered.

ROMANS 8:26

172.

Praying always with all prayer and
supplication in the Spirit, and watching
thereunto with all perseverance and
supplication for all saints.

EPHESIANS 6:18

173.

But ye, beloved, building up yourselves on
your most holy faith, praying in the Holy Ghost.

JUDE 1:20

174.

Then Peter said unto them, Repent, and be
baptized every one of you in the name of
Jesus Christ for the remission of sins, and ye
shall receive the gift of the Holy Ghost.

ACTS 2:38

175.

For we are saved by hope: but hope that is seen
is not hope: for what a man seeth, why doth he
yet hope for? But if we hope for that we see not,
then do we with patience wait for it.

ROMANS 8:24–25

176.

God is a Spirit: and they that worship him
must worship him in spirit and in truth.

JOHN 4:24

177.

And when ye stand praying, forgive, if ye have
ought against any: that your Father also which
is in heaven may forgive you your trespasses.

MARK 11:25

178.

What is it then? I will pray with the spirit,
and I will pray with the understanding also:
I will sing with the spirit, and I will sing
with the understanding also.

1 CORINTHIANS 14:15

179.

And be not drunk with wine, wherein is excess; but be filled with the Spirit.

EPHESIANS 5:18

———•◆•———

180.

That the righteousness of the law might be fulfilled in us, who walk not after the flesh, but after the Spirit.

ROMANS 8:4

PRAYING FOR CHILDREN

*Lord, You love children. When You walked on earth,
You valued them and called them near to You. You laid
hands on them and prayed to the Father on their behalf.
Please hear my prayers for all the children in my life.
This world is a dark place, and it is increasingly harder
to stand for Your ways and Your truths. I ask You to
strengthen these young ones spiritually. You promise
us in Your Word that there will always be a remnant
of Your people. How I pray my little loved ones will be
among that group of believers. Amen.*

181.

Lo, children are an heritage of the LORD:
and the fruit of the womb is his reward.

PSALM 127:3

182.

Take heed that ye despise not one of these
little ones; for I say unto you, That in
heaven their angels do always behold the
face of my Father which is in heaven.

MATTHEW 18:10

183.

And they brought unto him also infants,
that he would touch them: but when his disciples
saw it, they rebuked them. But Jesus called them
unto him, and said, Suffer little children to
come unto me, and forbid them not: for of such
is the kingdom of God. Verily I say unto you,
Whosoever shall not receive the kingdom of God
as a little child shall in no wise enter therein.

LUKE 18:15–17

184.

Train up a child in the way he should go:
and when he is old, he will not depart from it.

PROVERBS 22:6

185.

And these words, which I command thee this
day, shall be in thine heart: And thou shalt teach
them diligently unto thy children, and shalt talk
of them when thou sittest in thine house, and
when thou walkest by the way, and when thou
liest down, and when thou risest up.

DEUTERONOMY 6:6–7

186.

Children's children are the crown of old men;
and the glory of children are their fathers.

PROVERBS 17:6

187.

Even a child is known by his doings, whether
his work be pure, and whether it be right.

PROVERBS 20:11

188.

At the same time came the disciples unto
Jesus, saying, Who is the greatest in the kingdom
of heaven? And Jesus called a little child unto
him, and set him in the midst of them, And said,
Verily I say unto you, Except ye be converted,
and become as little children, ye shall not enter
into the kingdom of heaven.

MATTHEW 18:1–3

189.

I have no greater joy than to hear
that my children walk in truth.

3 JOHN 1:4

——————•◦•——————

190.

And he took a child, and set him in the midst
of them: and when he had taken him in his
arms, he said unto them, Whosoever shall
receive one of such children in my name,
receiveth me: and whosoever shall receive me,
receiveth not me, but him that sent me.

MARK 9:36–37

PRAYING SCRIPTURE

Heavenly Father, I love Your Word. When I pray through scripture, I am strengthened and encouraged by inserting my own name into the text, making Your promises personal to me. You, Father, have begun a good work in me. Christ died for me while I was yet a sinner. And I can be strong and courageous, as You commanded others to be through the ages. I thank You for scriptures and the ability to grow in my prayer life as I pray Your holy Word back to You. In Jesus' name I pray, amen.

191.

But God commendeth his love toward us, in that, while we were yet sinners, Christ died for us. Much more then, being now justified by his blood, we shall be saved from wrath through him. For if, when we were enemies, we were reconciled to God by the death of his Son, much more, being reconciled, we shall be saved by his life. And not only so, but we also joy in God through our Lord Jesus Christ, by whom we have now received the atonement.

ROMANS 5:8–11

192.

Being confident of this very thing, that he
which hath begun a good work in you will
perform it until the day of Jesus Christ.

<small>PHILIPPIANS 1:6</small>

193.

But now thus saith the LORD that created thee,
O Jacob, and he that formed thee, O Israel,
Fear not: for I have redeemed thee, I have called
thee by thy name; thou art mine. When thou
passest through the waters, I will be with thee;
and through the rivers, they shall not overflow
thee: when thou walkest through the fire,
thou shalt not be burned; neither shall
the flame kindle upon thee.

<small>ISAIAH 43:1–2</small>

194.

Then the word of the LORD came unto me,
saying, Before I formed thee in the belly I
knew thee; and before thou camest forth out
of the womb I sanctified thee, and I ordained
thee a prophet unto the nations.

<small>JEREMIAH 1:4–5</small>

195.

Have not I commanded thee? Be strong and of a good courage; be not afraid, neither be thou dismayed: for the LORD thy God is with thee whithersoever thou goest.

JOSHUA 1:9

196.

Now therefore ye are no more strangers and foreigners, but fellow citizens with the saints, and of the household of God.

EPHESIANS 2:19

197.

For the eyes of the LORD run to and fro throughout the whole earth, to shew himself strong in the behalf of them whose heart is perfect toward him. Herein thou hast done foolishly: therefore from henceforth thou shalt have wars.

2 CHRONICLES 16:9

198.

Let Israel hope in the LORD: for with
the LORD there is mercy, and with him
is plenteous redemption. And he shall
redeem Israel from all his iniquities.

PSALM 130:7–8

199.

The LORD shall fight for you,
and ye shall hold your peace.

EXODUS 14:14

200.

He giveth power to the faint; and to them
that have no might he increaseth strength.

ISAIAH 40:29

PRAYING THE PSALMS

*Lord, as I pray the psalms, I am awestruck that songs
written so long ago apply perfectly to my life today.
I discover new ways to praise You, seek You, and know
You better as I read these ancient words and make
them my own prayers. Guide me, Holy Spirit, as I
pray through the psalms. May I meditate on what the
words truly mean to my life and my faith. May praise,
glory, and honor take root in my heart as I pray. Amen.*

201.

Hear, O Lord, and have mercy upon me:
Lord, be thou my helper. Thou hast turned
for me my mourning into dancing: thou hast
put off my sackcloth, and girded me with
gladness; To the end that my glory may sing
praise to thee, and not be silent. O Lord my
God, I will give thanks unto thee for ever.

Psalm 30:10–12

202.

The heavens declare the glory of God;
and the firmament sheweth his handywork.

Psalm 19:1

203.

Why art thou cast down, O my soul?
and why art thou disquieted in me? hope
thou in God: for I shall yet praise him
for the help of his countenance.

Psalm 42:5

204.

Have mercy upon me, O God, according to thy
lovingkindness: according unto the multitude of
thy tender mercies blot out my transgressions.
Wash me throughly from mine iniquity,
and cleanse me from my sin.

Psalm 51:1–2

205.

I will praise thee; for I am fearfully and wonder-
fully made: marvellous are thy works; and that
my soul knoweth right well. My substance was
not hid from thee, when I was made in secret,
and curiously wrought in the lowest parts of the
earth. Thine eyes did see my substance, yet being
unperfect; and in thy book all my members were
written, which in continuance were fashioned,
when as yet there was none of them.

Psalm 139:14–16

206.

He restoreth my soul: he leadeth me in the paths
of righteousness for his name's sake. Yea, though
I walk through the valley of the shadow of
death, I will fear no evil: for thou art with me;
thy rod and thy staff they comfort me.

Psalm 23:3–4

207.

He that dwelleth in the secret place of the most
High shall abide under the shadow of the
Almighty. I will say of the Lord, He is my refuge
and my fortress: my God; in him will I trust.

Psalm 91:1–2

208.

The Lord is gracious, and full of compassion;
slow to anger, and of great mercy. The Lord
is good to all: and his tender mercies are over
all his works. All thy works shall praise thee,
O Lord; and thy saints shall bless thee.

Psalm 145:8–10

209.

One thing have I desired of the LORD, that will
I seek after; that I may dwell in the house of
the LORD all the days of my life, to behold the
beauty of the LORD, and to enquire in his temple.

PSALM 27:4

210.

The LORD is nigh unto them that are of a broken
heart; and saveth such as be of a contrite spirit.

PSALM 34:18

PRAYING IN THE MORNING

*Lord, early in the morning, before the world is busy
and bustling with noise all around me, I seek Your face.
Meet me here in the quiet. Calm my spirit. As I lay my
requests and concerns before You, remind me also to
listen for Your still, small voice. I want to be led and
assured and comforted by Your hand. I will seek You
and follow You throughout the day. Amen.*

211.

My voice shalt thou hear in the morning,
O Lord; in the morning will I direct my
prayer unto thee, and will look up.

Psalm 5:3

212.

It is of the Lord's mercies that we are not
consumed, because his compassions
fail not. They are new every morning:
great is thy faithfulness.

Lamentations 3:22–23

213.

Evening, and morning, and at noon, will I pray,
and cry aloud: and he shall hear my voice.

PSALM 55:17

214.

And in the morning, rising up a great while
before day, he went out, and departed into
a solitary place, and there prayed.

MARK 1:35

215.

For his anger endureth but a moment; in his
favour is life: weeping may endure for a
night, but joy cometh in the morning.

PSALM 30:5

216.

Cause me to hear thy lovingkindness in
the morning; for in thee do I trust: cause me
to know the way wherein I should walk;
for I lift up my soul unto thee.

PSALM 143:8

217.

O satisfy us early with thy mercy; that we
may rejoice and be glad all our days.

PSALM 90:14

218.

I prevented the dawning of the morning,
and cried: I hoped in thy word.

PSALM 119:147

219.

Awake up, my glory; awake, psaltery and harp:
I myself will awake early. I will praise thee,
O Lord, among the people: I will sing
unto thee among the nations.

PSALM 57:8–9

220.

And Abraham gat up early in the morning to
the place where he stood before the LORD.

GENESIS 19:27

PRAYING EARNESTLY

Dear God, may my prayers be overflowing with zeal and determination. Your Word declares that when Your children humble themselves and pray, You hear them. . . You forgive and heal. Your Word also promises that the fervent prayer of one who is righteous will profit much. I am righteous only through Christ, Father. And because I come to You through Him, I am confident that my earnest prayers will be heard and answered. In Jesus' name, amen.

221.
And ye shall seek me, and find me, when ye shall search for me with all your heart.

JEREMIAH 29:13

222.
If my people, which are called by my name, shall humble themselves, and pray, and seek my face, and turn from their wicked ways; then will I hear from heaven, and will forgive their sin, and will heal their land.

2 CHRONICLES 7:14

229.
the end of all things is at hand: be ye erefore sober, and watch unto prayer.

1 PETER 4:7

230.
e eyes of the Lord are over the righteous, s ears are open unto their prayers: but the of the Lord is against them that do evil.

1 PETER 3:12

223.

Blessed are they that keep his testimonies,
and that seek him with the whole heart.

Psalm 119:2

———•·•———

224.

Give me understanding, and I shall keep thy law;
yea, I shall observe it with my whole heart.

Psalm 119:34

———•·•———

225.

As many as I love, I rebuke and chasten:
be zealous therefore, and repent.

Revelation 3:19

226

O lord God of my salvatio
night before thee: Let m
thee: incline thine e

Psalm 88

———•·•

227.

Seek the Lord and
seek his face co

1 Chronicles

———•·•

228.

Because he hath incline
therefore will I call upon

Psalm 11

B
t

For
and
fa

PRAYING TOGETHER

Heavenly Father, You assure us in Your Word that You draw near when two or more are gathered in Your name. You hear our cries, and You will answer our prayers. Bless me, Father, with those who will pray with me. Give me a desire to pray with my significant other or a close friend. May I take the initiative and not be afraid to suggest that we stop and pray "in the moment" for needs as they arise. There is power in prayers offered together in the name of Jesus. Amen.

231.

These all continued with one accord in prayer and supplication, with the women, and Mary the mother of Jesus, and with his brethren.

Acts 1:14

232.

Now the God of patience and consolation grant you to be likeminded one toward another according to Christ Jesus: That ye may with one mind and one mouth glorify God, even the Father of our Lord Jesus Christ.

Romans 15:5–6

233.

I will therefore that men pray every where, lifting
up holy hands, without wrath and doubting.

1 Timothy 2:8

234.

And they continued stedfastly in
the apostles' doctrine and fellowship,
and in breaking of bread, and in prayers.

Acts 2:42

235.

For where two or three are gathered together
in my name, there am I in the midst of them.

Matthew 18:20

236.

And it came to pass about an eight days after
these sayings, he took Peter and John and
James, and went up into a mountain to pray.

LUKE 9:28

237.

And when he had considered the thing,
he came to the house of Mary the mother
of John, whose surname was Mark; where
many were gathered together praying.

ACTS 12:12

238.

And when the day of Pentecost was fully come,
they were all with one accord in one place.

ACTS 2:1

239.

And if one prevail against him,
two shall withstand him; and a
threefold cord is not quickly broken.

Ecclesiastes 4:12

240.

And let us consider one another to provoke unto
love and to good works: Not forsaking the
assembling of ourselves together, as the manner
of some is; but exhorting one another: and so
much the more, as ye see the day approaching.

Hebrews 10:24–25

PRAYING PRIVATELY

Lord, there is power in praying with others. But there are times when I must come to You all alone—just my Maker and me. Servant before Master. A child at the Father's feet. One day I must stand before You on my own. No one else can believe for me. And so I must learn to humbly bow before You and pray. Give me the words, Lord, and hear my heart when the words won't come. I seek to grow in private prayer, Father. In Jesus' name I pray, amen.

241.

On the morrow, as they went on their journey, and drew nigh unto the city, Peter went up upon the housetop to pray about the sixth hour.

Acts 10:9

242.

For we must all appear before the judgment seat of Christ; that every one may receive the things done in his body, according to that he hath done, whether it be good or bad.

2 Corinthians 5:10

243.

And he withdrew himself into
the wilderness, and prayed.

Luke 5:16

244.

But thou, when thou prayest, enter into thy
closet, and when thou hast shut thy door, pray
to thy Father which is in secret; and thy Father
which seeth in secret shall reward thee openly.

Matthew 6:6

245.

And it came to pass, as he was alone praying,
his disciples were with him: and he asked them,
saying, Whom say the people that I am?

Luke 9:18

246.

When Jesus heard of it, he departed thence
by ship into a desert place apart: and when
the people had heard thereof, they followed
him on foot out of the cities.

MATTHEW 14:13

247.

Wherefore the Lord said, Forasmuch as
this people draw near me with their mouth,
and with their lips do honour me, but have
removed their heart far from me, and their fear
toward me is taught by the precept of men.

ISAIAH 29:13

248.

Hear my cry, O God;
attend unto my prayer.

PSALM 61:1

249.

My soul, wait thou only upon God;
for my expectation is from him.
He only is my rock and my salvation:
he is my defence; I shall not be moved.

PSALM 62:5–6

250.

But without faith it is impossible to please
him: for he that cometh to God must
believe that he is, and that he is a rewarder
of them that diligently seek him.

HEBREWS 11:6

PRAYING FOR GOD'S WILL

Heavenly Father, I long to do Your will. I want to know that I am not missing out on Your perfect plan for me. Show me how to pray in such a way that Your will is revealed to me. I know that Your answers are not always immediate, so please give me patience as I wait for my future to unfold. I want to use every gift, talent, and resource You have blessed me with to do Your will. Help me to seek Your will all the days of my life. Amen.

251.

In every thing give thanks: for this is the will of God in Christ Jesus concerning you.

1 Thessalonians 5:18

252.

Now the God of peace, that brought again from the dead our Lord Jesus, that great shepherd of the sheep, through the blood of the everlasting covenant, Make you perfect in every good work to do his will, working in you that which is well pleasing in his sight, through Jesus Christ; to whom be glory for ever and ever. Amen.

Hebrews 13:20–21

253.

Thy word is a lamp unto my feet,
and a light unto my path.

PSALM 119:105

254.

For ye have need of patience, that,
after ye have done the will of God,
ye might receive the promise.

HEBREWS 10:36

255.

See then that ye walk circumspectly, not as fools,
but as wise, Redeeming the time, because
the days are evil. Wherefore be ye not unwise,
but understanding what the will of the Lord is.

EPHESIANS 5:15–17

256.

That the Lord thy God may shew
us the way wherein we may walk,
and the thing that we may do.

Jeremiah 42:3

257.

Teach me to do thy will; for thou art my
God: thy spirit is good; lead me into
the land of uprightness.

Psalm 143:10

258.

For whosoever shall do the will of God, the same
is my brother, and my sister, and mother.

Mark 3:35

259.

For I know the thoughts that I think toward
you, saith the LORD, thoughts of peace,
and not of evil, to give you an expected end.

JEREMIAH 29:11

260.

And he said to them all, If any man will come
after me, let him deny himself, and take
up his cross daily, and follow me.

LUKE 9:23

PRAYING THE NAMES AND ATTRIBUTES OF GOD

God, help me to know and understand You better. You are the Almighty and Sovereign God, but at the same time You say I may call You Abba (Daddy). As I study Your Word, I discover that You have many names and many attributes. You are the Provider, the Healer, my Peace, and a Banner over me. May I grow in my prayer life as I address You by Your holy names and marvel at Your lovingkindness, compassion, and power. Amen.

261.

And God said unto Moses, I AM THAT I AM:
and he said, Thus shalt thou say unto the
children of Israel, I AM hath sent me unto you.

EXODUS 3:14

262.

And the LORD said unto him, Peace be unto
thee; fear not: thou shalt not die. Then Gideon
built an altar there unto the LORD, and called
it Jehovahshalom: unto this day it is yet
in Ophrah of the Abiezrites.

JUDGES 6:23–24

263.

And the LORD said unto Moses, Write this for a memorial in a book, and rehearse it in the ears of Joshua: for I will utterly put out the remembrance of Amalek from under heaven. And Moses built an altar, and called the name of it Jehovahnissi.

EXODUS 17:14–15

264.

For ye have not received the spirit of bondage again to fear; but ye have received the Spirit of adoption, whereby we cry, Abba, Father.

ROMANS 8:15

265.

And she called the name of the LORD that spake unto her, Thou God seest me: for she said, Have I also here looked after him that seeth me?

GENESIS 16:13

266.

Blessed be God, even the Father of our Lord
Jesus Christ, the Father of mercies, and the God
of all comfort; Who comforteth us in all our
tribulation, that we may be able to comfort
them which are in any trouble, by the comfort
wherewith we ourselves are comforted of God.

2 Corinthians 1:3–4

267.

He that dwelleth in the secret place
of the most High shall abide under
the shadow of the Almighty.

Psalm 91:1

268.

And Abraham called the name of that place
Jehovahjireh: as it is said to this day, In the
mount of the Lord it shall be seen.

Genesis 22:14

269.

And said, If thou wilt diligently hearken to the
voice of the LORD thy God, and wilt do that
which is right in his sight, and wilt give ear to
his commandments, and keep all his statutes,
I will put none of these diseases upon thee,
which I have brought upon the Egyptians:
for I am the LORD that healeth thee.

EXODUS 15:26

270.

And he is before all things,
and by him all things consist.

COLOSSIANS 1:17

PRAYERS FOR STRENGTH

Heavenly Father, I remember the words I sang as a child: "Jesus loves me—this I know, for the Bible tells me so. Little ones to Him belong. They are weak, but He is strong." I am no longer a child, but wow, do those words bring me comfort! Be my strength as I face times of utter weakness—physically, mentally, emotionally, and spiritually. In Jesus' name I pray, amen.

271.

I can do all things through
Christ which strengtheneth me.

PHILIPPIANS 4:13

272.

Then he said unto them, Go your way, eat the fat, and drink the sweet, and send portions unto them for whom nothing is prepared: for this day is holy unto our LORD: neither be ye sorry; for the joy of the LORD is your strength.

NEHEMIAH 8:10

273.

The LORD is my strength and song, and he
is become my salvation: he is my God,
and I will prepare him an habitation;
my father's God, and I will exalt him.

EXODUS 15:2

274.

For thus saith the Lord GOD, the Holy One
of Israel; In returning and rest shall ye be
saved; in quietness and in confidence shall
be your strength: and ye would not.

ISAIAH 30:15

275.

The righteous cry, and the LORD heareth,
and delivereth them out of all their troubles.

PSALM 34:17

276.

Have not I commanded thee? Be strong and
of a good courage; be not afraid, neither be
thou dismayed: for the LORD thy God is
with thee whithersoever thou goest.

JOSHUA 1:9

277.

And he said unto me, My grace is sufficient
for thee: for my strength is made perfect in
weakness. Most gladly therefore will I rather
glory in my infirmities, that the power
of Christ may rest upon me.

2 CORINTHIANS 12:9

278.

Now the Lord of peace himself give you peace
always by all means. The Lord be with you all.

2 THESSALONIANS 3:16

279.

Wait on the Lord: be of good courage,
and he shall strengthen thine heart:
wait, I say, on the Lord.

PSALM 27:14

280.

Wisdom strengtheneth the wise more than
ten mighty men which are in the city.

ECCLESIASTES 7:19

PRAYERS FOR HEALING

Great Physician, I ask You for healing for myself and for others. You create all life, and You sustain it. Your ways are mysterious and far above my own. I long for healing in the here and now. I would love for You to remove the pain. But I pray first and foremost for Your will. I know that one day there will be a perfect healing. In heaven, the lame will walk and the blind will see. There will be no more sorrow and no more crying. And so, for today, I earnestly ask for healing; but above all, I seek Your will. In Jesus' powerful name I pray, amen.

281.

Heal me, O LORD, and I shall be healed; save me, and I shall be saved: for thou art my praise.

JEREMIAH 17:14

282.

Surely he hath borne our griefs, and carried our sorrows: yet we did esteem him stricken, smitten of God, and afflicted. But he was wounded for our transgressions, he was bruised for our iniquities: the chastisement of our peace was upon him; and with his stripes we are healed.

ISAIAH 53:4–5

283.

For I will restore health unto thee, and I
will heal thee of thy wounds, saith the LORD;
because they called thee an Outcast, saying,
This is Zion, whom no man seeketh after.

JEREMIAH 30:17

284.

Beloved, I wish above all things that thou
mayest prosper and be in health,
even as thy soul prospereth.

3 JOHN 2

285.

And God shall wipe away all tears from their eyes;
and there shall be no more death, neither sorrow,
nor crying, neither shall there be any more pain:
for the former things are passed away.

REVELATION 21:4

286.

O Lord my God, I cried unto thee,
and thou hast healed me.

Psalm 30:2

287.

Bless the Lord, O my soul, and forget not
all his benefits: Who forgiveth all thine
iniquities; who healeth all thy diseases.

Psalm 103:2–3

288.

Hear, O Lord, and have mercy upon me: Lord,
be thou my helper. Thou hast turned for me my
mourning into dancing: thou hast put off my
sackcloth, and girded me with gladness.

Psalm 30:10–11

289.

My flesh and my heart faileth: but God is the
strength of my heart, and my portion for ever.

PSALM 73:26

290.

When Jesus heard it, he saith unto them,
They that are whole have no need of the
physician, but they that are sick: I came not to
call the righteous, but sinners to repentance.

MARK 2:17

PRAYERS FOR PROTECTION

God, I am thankful for Your protection. I know You have appointed Your angels to watch over me. I pray that You would protect my heart and mind as well as my body. There is so much darkness in the world today, and I ask that You would keep me safe in Your holy light. I cry out to You to save me from paths and people who would seek to destroy me. I pray also for the protection of my loved ones and of Your Church. In Jesus' name I pray, amen.

291.

For thou, LORD, wilt bless the righteous; with favour wilt thou compass him as with a shield.

PSALM 5:12

292.

Deliver me from mine enemies, O my God: defend me from them that rise up against me.

PSALM 59:1

293.

But let all those that put their trust in thee
rejoice: let them ever shout for joy, because
thou defendest them: let them also that
love thy name be joyful in thee.

PSALM 5:11

294.

There hath no temptation taken you but such as
is common to man: but God is faithful, who will
not suffer you to be tempted above that ye are
able; but will with the temptation also make a
way to escape, that ye may be able to bear it.

1 CORINTHIANS 10:13

295.

Fear thou not; for I am with thee: be not
dismayed; for I am thy God: I will strengthen
thee; yea, I will help thee; yea, I will uphold
thee with the right hand of my righteousness.

ISAIAH 41:10

296.

Be merciful unto me, O God, be merciful unto
me: for my soul trusteth in thee: yea, in the
shadow of thy wings will I make my refuge,
until these calamities be overpast.

PSALM 57:1

297.

And I give unto them eternal life; and they
shall never perish, neither shall any man pluck
them out of my hand. My Father, which gave
them me, is greater than all; and no man is able
to pluck them out of my Father's hand.

JOHN 10:28–29

298.

Yea, though I walk through the valley of the
shadow of death, I will fear no evil: for thou art
with me; thy rod and thy staff they comfort me.
Thou preparest a table before me in the presence
of mine enemies: thou anointest my head
with oil; my cup runneth over.

PSALM 23:4–5

299.

For he shall give his angels charge over thee,
to keep thee in all thy ways. They shall
bear thee up in their hands, lest thou
dash thy foot against a stone.

PSALM 91:11–12

300.

I will both lay me down in peace, and sleep:
for thou, LORD, only makest me dwell in safety.

PSALM 4:8

PRAYERS FOR COURAGE

Mighty God, I know You are steadfast and true. Give me courage to face those who question my faith and mock the choices I make as I seek to follow You. Give me courage to run my household in a godly manner. Give me strength to step out in faith to live and serve as You call me to do. I need Your help to confidently face the unknown. I know You will grow my faith as I continue to trust You to make me brave. Amen.

301.

Therefore, my beloved brethren, be ye stedfast,
unmoveable, always abounding in the work
of the Lord, forasmuch as ye know that
your labour is not in vain in the Lord.

1 CORINTHIANS 15:58

302.

Finally, my brethren, be strong in the Lord,
and in the power of his might.

EPHESIANS 6:10

303.

Fear not; for thou shalt not be ashamed: neither
be thou confounded; for thou shalt not be put
to shame: for thou shalt forget the shame of thy
youth, and shalt not remember the reproach
of thy widowhood any more.

ISAIAH 54:4

304.

For God hath not given us the spirit of fear;
but of power, and of love, and of a sound mind.

2 TIMOTHY 1:7

305.

Watch ye, stand fast in the faith,
quit you like men, be strong.

1 CORINTHIANS 16:13

306.

As soon as Jesus heard the word that was spoken, he saith unto the ruler of the synagogue, Be not afraid, only believe.

MARK 5:36

307.

He shall not be afraid of evil tidings: his heart is fixed, trusting in the LORD.

PSALM 112:7

308.

Be of good courage, and he shall strengthen your heart, all ye that hope in the LORD.

PSALM 31:24

309.

Be strong and of a good courage, fear not,
nor be afraid of them: for the LORD thy
God, he it is that doth go with thee;
he will not fail thee, nor forsake thee.

DEUTERONOMY 31:6

———————•◦•———————

310.

I have set the LORD always before me: because
he is at my right hand, I shall not be moved.

PSALM 16:8

PRAYERS OF CONFESSION

Lord, I confess my sins and seek Your forgiveness. I know that only through Christ Jesus am I able to stand before You in this manner. He died once—and He died for all mankind. And through faith, I have accepted His gift of salvation. Strengthen me as I repent. Help me to turn fully from the sins that so easily ensnare me. I am a sinner, saved only by Your grace. In the name of Jesus I pray, amen.

311.

He that covereth his sins shall not prosper:
but whoso confesseth and forsaketh
them shall have mercy.

PROVERBS 28:13

312.

I acknowledge my sin unto thee, and mine
iniquity have I not hid. I said, I will confess
my transgressions unto the LORD; and thou
forgavest the iniquity of my sin. Selah.

PSALM 32:5

313.

Repent ye therefore, and be converted,
that your sins may be blotted out,
when the times of refreshing shall
come from the presence of the Lord.

Acts 3:19

314.

For with the heart man believeth unto
righteousness; and with the mouth
confession is made unto salvation.

Romans 10:10

315.

For all have sinned, and come short of the glory
of God; Being justified freely by his grace through
the redemption that is in Christ Jesus.

Romans 3:23–24

316.

When I kept silence, my bones waxed
old through my roaring all the day long.

PSALM 32:3

317.

That if thou shalt confess with thy mouth
the Lord Jesus, and shalt believe in thine
heart that God hath raised him from
the dead, thou shalt be saved.

ROMANS 10:9

318.

If we confess our sins, he is faithful
and just to forgive us our sins, and to
cleanse us from all unrighteousness.

1 JOHN 1:9

319.
And he is the propitiation for our sins:
and not for ours only, but also for
the sins of the whole world.

1 John 2:2

320.
Then Peter said unto them, Repent, and be
baptized every one of you in the name of
Jesus Christ for the remission of sins, and ye
shall receive the gift of the Holy Ghost.

Acts 2:38

PAUL'S PRAYERS

Father, as I read and dwell upon the prayers of the apostle Paul, an amazing preacher of the Good News, I find strength for my own prayer life. I read his prayers for himself and for others, and his earnest prayers for many to come to know Christ. Cause my heart to long for prayer so deeply that I will make it a regular part of each and every day. May I pray like Paul prayed, and may I see the results in my own life. Amen.

321.
And I thank Christ Jesus our Lord,
who hath enabled me, for that he counted
me faithful, putting me into the ministry.
1 Timothy 1:12

322.
For this thing I besought the Lord thrice,
that it might depart from me. And he said
unto me, My grace is sufficient for thee: for my
strength is made perfect in weakness. Most gladly
therefore will I rather glory in my infirmities,
that the power of Christ may rest upon me.
2 Corinthians 12:8–9

323.

The Lord Jesus Christ be with thy spirit.
Grace be with you. Amen.

2 TIMOTHY 4:22

324.

Now thanks be unto God, which always causeth
us to triumph in Christ, and maketh manifest
the savour of his knowledge by us in every place.
For we are unto God a sweet savour of Christ,
in them that are saved, and in them that perish:
To the one we are the savour of death unto death;
and to the other the savour of life unto life.
And who is sufficient for these things?

2 CORINTHIANS 2:14–16

325.

Blessed be the God and Father of our Lord Jesus
Christ, who hath blessed us with all spiritual
blessings in heavenly places in Christ.

EPHESIANS 1:3

326.

To the end he may stablish your hearts
unblameable in holiness before God,
even our Father, at the coming of our
Lord Jesus Christ with all his saints.

1 Thessalonians 3:13

327.

Hearing of thy love and faith, which thou hast
toward the Lord Jesus, and toward all saints;
That the communication of thy faith may become
effectual by the acknowledging of every good
thing which is in you in Christ Jesus.

Philemon 5–6

328.

Brethren, my heart's desire and prayer to
God for Israel is, that they might be saved.

Romans 10:1

329.

Wherefore I also, after I heard of your faith in
the Lord Jesus, and love unto all the saints,
Cease not to give thanks for you, making
mention of you in my prayers.

EPHESIANS 1:15–16

330.

First, I thank my God through Jesus
Christ for you all, that your faith is spoken
of throughout the whole world. For God is my
witness, whom I serve with my spirit in the
gospel of his Son, that without ceasing I make
mention of you always in my prayers.

ROMANS 1:8–9

PRAYERS OF THANKFULNESS

Lord, thank You. Thank You for creating and saving me. Thank You for all the blessings in my life. Thank You for the times when my prayers seem to go unanswered, for I can often see later that what I desired would not have been best for me! You are a good, good Father, and I praise You for who You are. Create in me a heart of thankfulness. Grow and nurture it that I might always take time each day to express my gratefulness to You. Amen.

331.

In every thing give thanks: for this is the will of God in Christ Jesus concerning you.

1 THESSALONIANS 5:18

332.

O give thanks unto the LORD, for he is good: for his mercy endureth for ever.

PSALM 107:1

333.

Giving thanks always for all things unto God and
the Father in the name of our Lord Jesus Christ.

EPHESIANS 5:20

334.

And let the peace of God rule in your hearts,
to the which also ye are called in one body;
and be ye thankful. Let the word of Christ
dwell in you richly in all wisdom; teaching and
admonishing one another in psalms and hymns
and spiritual songs, singing with grace in your
hearts to the Lord. And whatsoever ye do in word
or deed, do all in the name of the Lord Jesus,
giving thanks to God and the Father by him.

COLOSSIANS 3:15–17

335.

Every good gift and every perfect gift is
from above, and cometh down from
the Father of lights, with whom is no
variableness, neither shadow of turning.

JAMES 1:17

336.

O give thanks unto the Lord; call upon his name:
make known his deeds among the people.

PSALM 105:1

337.

O give thanks unto the Lord; for he is good:
because his mercy endureth for ever.

PSALM 118:1

338.

Know ye that the Lord he is God: it is he
that hath made us, and not we ourselves;
we are his people, and the sheep of his
pasture. Enter into his gates with thanksgiving,
and into his courts with praise: be thankful
unto him, and bless his name. For the Lord
is good; his mercy is everlasting; and his
truth endureth to all generations.

PSALM 100:3–5

339.

I will praise thee, O Lord, with my whole heart;
I will shew forth all thy marvellous works. I will
be glad and rejoice in thee: I will sing praise
to thy name, O thou most High.

Psalm 9:1–2

———————•◦•———————

340.

And in that day shall ye say, Praise the Lord, call
upon his name, declare his doings among the
people, make mention that his name is exalted.
Sing unto the Lord; for he hath done excellent
things: this is known in all the earth.

Isaiah 12:4–5

LISTENING TO GOD

*Father, I often come before You with just a few free
minutes, and I rattle off my list of requests to You in
prayer. I need to slow down and listen to You! I know
prayer should not be all about what I have to say.
You are the God of the universe—and I have the
opportunity and the privilege to come to You in prayer.
May I take time to rest and be still. Only then will I
be able to truly hear what You have to say to me. Make
me a better listener, I pray. May I begin today. Amen.*

341.
My son, if thou wilt receive my words,
and hide my commandments with thee;
So that thou incline thine ear unto wisdom,
and apply thine heart to understanding; Yea,
if thou criest after knowledge, and liftest up
thy voice for understanding; If thou seekest
her as silver, and searchest for her as for hid
treasures; Then shalt thou understand the fear
of the LORD, and find the knowledge of God.
PROVERBS 2:1–5

342.

My sheep hear my voice, and I know them,
and they follow me: And I give unto them
eternal life; and they shall never perish, neither
shall any man pluck them out of my hand.

JOHN 10:27–28

343.

Behold, I stand at the door, and knock:
if any man hear my voice, and open the
door, I will come in to him, and will
sup with him, and he with me.

REVELATION 3:20

344.

But be ye doers of the word, and not
hearers only, deceiving your own selves.

JAMES 1:22

345.

He that is of God heareth God's words.

John 8:47

346.

Ye shall walk after the Lord your God,
and fear him, and keep his commandments,
and obey his voice, and ye shall serve him,
and cleave unto him.

Deuteronomy 13:4

347.

All scripture is given by inspiration of God,
and is profitable for doctrine, for reproof,
for correction, for instruction in righteousness.

2 Timothy 3:16

348.

The way of a fool is right in his own eyes:
but he that hearkeneth unto counsel is wise.

PROVERBS 12:15

349.

My soul, wait thou only upon God; for my
expectation is from him. He only is my
rock and my salvation: he is my defence;
I shall not be moved.

PSALM 62:5–6

350.

Hear, O my people, and I will testify unto thee:
O Israel, if thou wilt hearken unto me.

PSALM 81:8

PRAYING FOR
SPIRITUAL GROWTH

*Heavenly Father, I do not want to become stagnant
in my spiritual walk. As I am seeking to grow in my
prayer life, I seek also to grow spiritually in every way.
May I place the highest priority on spending time in
Your Word, in prayer, and with Your people. I learn so
much when I follow through on these things, and I can
tell I am maturing spiritually. Thank You for hearing
my prayers to increase my faith and my knowledge.
I love You, Lord, and I want to walk closer and closer
with You every day of my life. Amen.*

351.

Therefore leaving the principles of the doctrine
of Christ, let us go on unto perfection;
not laying again the foundation of repentance
from dead works, and of faith toward God.

HEBREWS 6:1

352.

And the child Samuel grew on, and was in
favour both with the LORD, and also with men.

1 SAMUEL 2:26

353.

But grow in grace, and in the knowledge of
our Lord and Saviour Jesus Christ. To him
be glory both now and for ever. Amen.

2 PETER 3:18

354.

As newborn babes, desire the sincere milk of
the word, that ye may grow thereby: If so be
ye have tasted that the Lord is gracious.

1 PETER 2:2–3

355.

For this cause we also, since the day we heard it,
do not cease to pray for you, and to desire that
ye might be filled with the knowledge of his
will in all wisdom and spiritual understanding;
That ye might walk worthy of the Lord unto all
pleasing, being fruitful in every good work,
and increasing in the knowledge of God.

COLOSSIANS 1:9–10

356.

And the apostles said unto the Lord,
Increase our faith.

Luke 17:5

357.

For every one that useth milk is unskilful in the
word of righteousness: for he is a babe. But strong
meat belongeth to them that are of full age, even
those who by reason of use have their senses
exercised to discern both good and evil.

Hebrews 5:13–14

358.

When I was a child, I spake as a child,
I understood as a child, I thought as a child:
but when I became a man, I put away childish
things. For now we see through a glass, darkly;
but then face to face: now I know in part; but
then shall I know even as also I am known.

1 Corinthians 13:11–12

359.

And Jesus said unto them, Because of your unbelief: for verily I say unto you, If ye have faith as a grain of mustard seed, ye shall say unto this mountain, Remove hence to yonder place; and it shall remove; and nothing shall be impossible unto you.

MATTHEW 17:20

360.

He that spared not his own Son, but delivered him up for us all, how shall he not with him also freely give us all things?

ROMANS 8:32

PRAYERS OF PRAISE

*Lord, You alone are worthy of all my praise. May I
praise Your name every day that You grant me life on
this earth. You are good and righteous. You alone are
God! As I praise You, I am reminded that I am a mere
human and You are divine. Even the breath in my lungs,
which I use to sing Your praise, has come directly from
You. I love You, Lord, and I know that praise honors You
and is, at the same time, so good for my soul! Amen.*

361.

It is a good thing to give thanks unto the LORD,
and to sing praises unto thy name, O Most High.

PSALM 92:1

362.

But ye are a chosen generation,
a royal priesthood, an holy nation,
a peculiar people; that ye should shew
forth the praises of him who hath called
you out of darkness into his marvellous light.

1 PETER 2:9

363.

Let every thing that hath breath
praise the LORD. Praise ye the LORD.

PSALM 150:6

364.

I will praise the LORD according to his
righteousness: and will sing praise
to the name of the LORD most high.

PSALM 7:17

365.

The LORD is my strength and my shield;
my heart trusted in him, and I am helped:
therefore my heart greatly rejoiceth;
and with my song will I praise him.

PSALM 28:7

366.

I will bless the LORD at all times:
his praise shall continually be in my mouth.

PSALM 34:1

367.

And he hath put a new song in my mouth,
even praise unto our God: many shall see it,
and fear, and shall trust in the LORD.

PSALM 40:3

368.

Why art thou cast down, O my soul?
and why art thou disquieted in me?
hope thou in God: for I shall yet praise
him for the help of his countenance.

PSALM 42:5

369.

O Lord, thou art my God; I will exalt
thee, I will praise thy name; for thou hast
done wonderful things; thy counsels of
old are faithfulness and truth.

Isaiah 25:1

370.

For the grave cannot praise thee, death can not
celebrate thee: they that go down into the pit
cannot hope for thy truth. The living, the living,
he shall praise thee, as I do this day: the father
to the children shall make known thy truth.

Isaiah 38:18–19

PRAYERS FOR BOLDNESS
TO SHARE THE GOSPEL

Lord, make me bold as I go into the world. Within my social circles, there are many who do not yet know You. Help me to be passionate about sharing Jesus with them. I recognize that without Him, there is no hope for salvation; and without salvation, the lost will spend eternity separated from You. Give me a sense of urgency! I pray You would give me greater courage, so sharing the Good News would soon be as natural for me as breathing. In Jesus' name I ask these things. Amen.

371.

According to the eternal purpose which
he purposed in Christ Jesus our Lord:
In whom we have boldness and access
with confidence by the faith of him.

Ephesians 3:11–12

372.

Then they that gladly received his word were
baptized: and the same day there were added
unto them about three thousand souls.

Acts 2:41

373.

And for me, that utterance may be given unto me, that I may open my mouth boldly, to make known the mystery of the gospel, For which I am an ambassador in bonds: that therein I may speak boldly, as I ought to speak.

EPHESIANS 6:19–20

374.

Withal praying also for us, that God would open unto us a door of utterance, to speak the mystery of Christ, for which I am also in bonds: That I may make it manifest, as I ought to speak.

COLOSSIANS 4:3–4

375.

And now, Lord, behold their threatenings: and grant unto thy servants, that with all boldness they may speak thy word, By stretching forth thine hand to heal; and that signs and wonders may be done by the name of thy holy child Jesus.

ACTS 4:29–30

376.

Praying always with all prayer and supplication
in the Spirit, and watching thereunto with
all perseverance and supplication for all saints.

EPHESIANS 6:18

377.

For I am not ashamed of the gospel of Christ:
for it is the power of God unto salvation to
every one that believeth; to the Jew first, and also
to the Greek. For therein is the righteousness
of God revealed from faith to faith: as it is
written, The just shall live by faith.

ROMANS 1:16–17

378.

So that we may boldly say, The Lord is my helper,
and I will not fear what man shall do unto me.

HEBREWS 13:6

379.

And he went into the synagogue, and spake
boldly for the space of three months,
disputing and persuading the things
concerning the kingdom of God.

ACTS 19:8

380.

And Jesus came and spake unto them, saying,
All power is given unto me in heaven and in
earth. Go ye therefore, and teach all nations,
baptizing them in the name of the Father,
and of the Son, and of the Holy Ghost: Teaching
them to observe all things whatsoever I have
commanded you: and, lo, I am with you always,
even unto the end of the world. Amen.

MATTHEW 28:18–20

PRAYERS FOR HEART TRANSFORMATION

Father, transform my heart. Give me a heart that is sensitive to spiritual things. Take my old heart, a heart of stone, and replace it with a heart that breaks for the same causes that also break Your heart. Forgive my sins. Lead me in a new path, a way that honors You and upholds Your statutes. Make me an instrument of Your peace and a vessel through which Your love is shown to others. In Jesus' name, I ask for a daily transforming and renewing of my mind. Amen.

381.

Create in me a clean heart, O God;
and renew a right spirit within me.

PSALM 51:10

382.

I am crucified with Christ: nevertheless I live; yet not I, but Christ liveth in me: and the life which I now live in the flesh I live by the faith of the Son of God, who loved me, and gave himself for me.

GALATIANS 2:20

383.

Keep thy heart with all diligence;
for out of it are the issues of life.

PROVERBS 4:23

384.

For a good tree bringeth not forth corrupt
fruit; neither doth a corrupt tree bring forth
good fruit. For every tree is known by his own
fruit. For of thorns men do not gather figs,
nor of a bramble bush gather they grapes.
A good man out of the good treasure of his heart
bringeth forth that which is good; and an evil
man out of the evil treasure of his heart bringeth
forth that which is evil: for of the abundance
of the heart his mouth speaketh.

LUKE 6:43–45

385.

I will put my spirit within you, and cause
you to walk in my statutes, and ye shall
keep my judgments, and do them.

EZEKIEL 36:27

386.

I beseech you therefore, brethren, by the mercies
of God, that ye present your bodies a living
sacrifice, holy, acceptable unto God, which is
your reasonable service. And be not conformed to
this world: but be ye transformed by the renewing
of your mind, that ye may prove what is that good,
and acceptable, and perfect, will of God.

ROMANS 12:1–2

387.

For God, who commanded the light to shine
out of darkness, hath shined in our hearts,
to give the light of the knowledge of the glory
of God in the face of Jesus Christ.

2 CORINTHIANS 4:6

388.

But we all, with open face beholding as in a
glass the glory of the Lord, are changed
into the same image from glory to glory,
even as by the Spirit of the Lord.

2 CORINTHIANS 3:18

389.

I will give them an heart to know me,
that I am the LORD: and they shall be my
people, and I will be their God: for they
shall return unto me with their whole heart.

JEREMIAH 24:7

390.

That ye put off concerning the former
conversation the old man, which is corrupt
according to the deceitful lusts; And be renewed
in the spirit of your mind; And that ye put on
the new man, which after God is created
in righteousness and true holiness.

EPHESIANS 4:22–24

PRAY WITHOUT PRETENSE

Dear Jesus, I read of the Pharisees' grandiose prayers in the Bible. You instructed people not to pray as they did. Show me how to pray, Lord, without being pretentious. I want to have a pure heart before You. I want to be humble and honest. Help me to always remember to be grateful to You for all You have done for me. Guide me even now as I pray. Amen.

391.

If we say that we have fellowship with him, and walk in darkness, we lie, and do not the truth: But if we walk in the light, as he is in the light, we have fellowship one with another, and the blood of Jesus Christ his Son cleanseth us from all sin.

1 John 1:6–7

392.

If we confess our sins, he is faithful and just to forgive us our sins, and to cleanse us from all unrighteousness. If we say that we have not sinned, we make him a liar, and his word is not in us.

1 John 1:9–10

393.

But woe unto you, scribes and Pharisees,
hypocrites! for ye shut up the kingdom of
heaven against men: for ye neither go in
yourselves, neither suffer ye them that are
entering to go in. Woe unto you, scribes and
Pharisees, hypocrites! for ye devour widows'
houses, and for a pretence make long prayer:
therefore ye shall receive the greater damnation.

MATTHEW 23:13–14

394.

For by grace are ye saved through faith;
and that not of yourselves: it is the gift of God:
Not of works, lest any man should boast.

EPHESIANS 2:8–9

395.

Be ye therefore followers of God, as dear children;
And walk in love, as Christ also hath loved us,
and hath given himself for us an offering and a
sacrifice to God for a sweetsmelling savour.

EPHESIANS 5:1–2

396.

For not the hearers of the law are just before God,
but the doers of the law shall be justified.

ROMANS 2:13

397.

Not every one that saith unto me, Lord,
Lord, shall enter into the kingdom of
heaven; but he that doeth the will of
my Father which is in heaven.

MATTHEW 7:21

398.

But when ye pray, use not vain repetitions,
as the heathen do: for they think that they
shall be heard for their much speaking.
Be not ye therefore like unto them:
for your Father knoweth what things
ye have need of, before ye ask him.

MATTHEW 6:7–8

399.

But he giveth more grace. Wherefore
he saith, God resisteth the proud,
but giveth grace unto the humble.

JAMES 4:6

400.

For whosoever exalteth himself shall be abased;
and he that humbleth himself shall be exalted.

LUKE 14:11

PRAY UNCEASINGLY

*Heavenly Father, You call me to pray without ceasing
and to give thanks in all circumstances. This is a tall
order! Place in me a spirit of prayer that travels
with me throughout my days. Help me to find many
moments to utter short prayers to You, asking You for
help in my decision-making, bringing a need before You,
offering a prayer of thanks. May this become the norm
for me. In Jesus' name I ask these things, amen.*

401.

Rejoice evermore. Pray without ceasing.
In every thing give thanks: for this is the
will of God in Christ Jesus concerning you.

1 Thessalonians 5:16–18

402.

Now when Daniel knew that the writing
was signed, he went into his house; and his
windows being open in his chamber toward
Jerusalem, he kneeled upon his knees three
times a day, and prayed, and gave thanks
before his God, as he did aforetime.

Daniel 6:10

403.

Rejoicing in hope; patient in tribulation;
continuing instant in prayer.

ROMANS 12:12

404.

Praying always with all prayer and supplication
in the Spirit, and watching thereunto with all
perseverance and supplication for all saints.

EPHESIANS 6:18

405.

Continue in prayer, and watch
in the same with thanksgiving.

COLOSSIANS 4:2

406.

By him therefore let us offer the sacrifice
of praise to God continually, that is, the fruit
of our lips giving thanks to his name.

HEBREWS 13:15

407.

Seven times a day do I praise thee
because of thy righteous judgments.

PSALM 119:164

408.

Be careful for nothing; but in every thing by
prayer and supplication with thanksgiving let
your requests be made known unto God.

PHILIPPIANS 4:6

409.
Call unto me, and I will answer thee,
and show thee great and mighty things,
which thou knowest not.

JEREMIAH 33:3

410.
If ye abide in me, and my words abide
in you, ye shall ask what ye will,
and it shall be done unto you.

JOHN 15:7

PRAYERS OF
SPIRITUAL WARFARE

*Heavenly Father, I am aware that there is another
realm—a spiritual realm—where not only good spirits
but evil ones exist. So I ask for Your protection of my
heart. I pray that You would keep me focused on Your
truth through my daily time with You, in Bible reading,
and in prayer. May nothing Satan throws at me be
strong enough to turn my eyes to the left or to the right.
Protect me, I pray, and use me for Your Kingdom's glory.
In Jesus' name I pray, amen.*

411.
Beloved, believe not every spirit, but try the
spirits whether they are of God: because many
false prophets are gone out into the world.
1 JOHN 4:1

412.
For we wrestle not against flesh and blood,
but against principalities, against powers, against
the rulers of the darkness of this world, against
spiritual wickedness in high places.
EPHESIANS 6:12

413.

He that dwelleth in the secret place of the
most High shall abide under the shadow of
the Almighty. I will say of the LORD, He is my
refuge and my fortress: my God; in him will
I trust. Surely he shall deliver thee from the
snare of the fowler, and from the noisome
pestilence. He shall cover thee with his feathers,
and under his wings shalt thou trust:
his truth shall be thy shield and buckler.

PSALM 91:1–4

414.

The LORD shall cause thine enemies that rise
up against thee to be smitten before thy face:
they shall come out against thee one way,
and flee before thee seven ways.

DEUTERONOMY 28:7

415.

For the weapons of our warfare are
not carnal, but mighty through God
to the pulling down of strong holds.

2 CORINTHIANS 10:4

416.

And ye shall know the truth,
and the truth shall make you free.

JOHN 8:32

417.

Casting down imaginations, and every high
thing that exalteth itself against the knowledge
of God, and bringing into captivity every
thought to the obedience of Christ.

2 CORINTHIANS 10:5

418.

Forasmuch then as the children are partakers
of flesh and blood, he also himself likewise
took part of the same; that through death he
might destroy him that had the power
of death, that is, the devil.

HEBREWS 2:14

419.
Ye are of God, little children, and have overcome
them: because greater is he that is in you,
than he that is in the world.
1 JOHN 4:4

420.
And the great dragon was cast out, that old
serpent, called the Devil, and Satan, which
deceiveth the whole world: he was cast out into
the earth, and his angels were cast out with him.
REVELATION 12:9

PRAYERS FOR THE LOST

Heavenly Father, I am so thankful that I have come to know Jesus as my Savior. Give me a burning passion to pray for those who are lost. They do not hear Your voice or know You as Lord, and yet they need You, Father! Cause my mind to dwell on the urgency for such prayers, and give me the right words. I long to see the lost come to know You! Amen.

421.

The Lord is not slack concerning his promise, as some men count slackness; but is longsuffering to us-ward, not willing that any should perish, but that all should come to repentance.

2 PETER 3:9

422.

To open their eyes, and to turn them from darkness to light, and from the power of Satan unto God, that they may receive forgiveness of sins, and inheritance among them which are sanctified by faith that is in me.

ACTS 26:18

423.

Then saith he unto his disciples, The harvest
truly is plenteous, but the labourers are few;
Pray ye therefore the Lord of the harvest, that
he will send forth labourers into his harvest.

MATTHEW 9:37–38

424.

Therefore will I divide him a portion with the
great, and he shall divide the spoil with the
strong; because he hath poured out his soul
unto death: and he was numbered with the
transgressors; and he bare the sin of many,
and made intercession for the transgressors.

ISAIAH 53:12

425.

No man can come to me, except the Father
which hath sent me draw him: and I will
raise him up at the last day.

JOHN 6:44

426.

I exhort therefore, that, first of all, supplications,
prayers, intercessions, and giving of thanks,
be made for all men; For kings, and for all that
are in authority; that we may lead a quiet and
peaceable life in all godliness and honesty.
For this is good and acceptable in the sight of God
our Saviour; Who will have all men to be saved,
and to come unto the knowledge of the truth.

1 Timothy 2:1–4

427.

But when he saw the multitudes,
he was moved with compassion on them,
because they fainted, and were scattered
abroad, as sheep having no shepherd.

Matthew 9:36

428.

For God so loved the world, that he gave his only
begotten Son, that whosoever believeth in him
should not perish, but have everlasting life.

John 3:16

429.

And that they may recover themselves
out of the snare of the devil, who are
taken captive by him at his will.

2 Timothy 2:26

430.

A new heart also will I give you, and a new
spirit will I put within you: and I will take
away the stony heart out of your flesh,
and I will give you an heart of flesh.

Ezekiel 36:26

PRAYERS OF
SUPPLICATION

God, so often I come before You in prayer for the needs of others. Remind me that You want me to cast my cares upon You as well. You are always there to hear my cries. You know my needs before I even speak them, but there is power in voicing my prayers to You. It gives me the chance to see You work! These are the most vulnerable of all my prayers because I must open up my heart to You and express my weaknesses and my needs. Father, hear my prayers for my own needs. In Jesus' name I pray, amen.

431.
Be careful for nothing; but in every thing by prayer and supplication with thanksgiving let your requests be made known unto God.

PHILIPPIANS 4:6

432.
Let us therefore come boldly unto the throne of grace, that we may obtain mercy, and find grace to help in time of need.

HEBREWS 4:16

433.

Casting all your care upon him;
for he careth for you.

1 PETER 5:7

434.

Grant thee according to thine own heart,
and fulfil all thy counsel. We will rejoice in thy
salvation, and in the name of our God we will set
up our banners: the LORD fulfil all thy petitions.

PSALM 20:4–5

435.

But my God shall supply all your need according
to his riches in glory by Christ Jesus.

PHILIPPIANS 4:19

436.

Hear the voice of my supplications,
when I cry unto thee, when I lift up
my hands toward thy holy oracle.

PSALM 28:2

437.

The LORD hath heard my supplication;
the LORD will receive my prayer.

PSALM 6:9

438.

Let my supplication come before thee:
deliver me according to thy word.

PSALM 119:170

439.

Bow down thine ear, O LORD, hear me:
for I am poor and needy. Preserve my soul;
for I am holy: O thou my God, save thy
servant that trusteth in thee. Be merciful
unto me, O Lord: for I cry unto thee daily.

PSALM 86:1–3

440.

And it was so, that when Solomon had
made an end of praying all this prayer and
supplication unto the LORD, he arose from
before the altar of the LORD, from kneeling on
his knees with his hands spread up to heaven.

1 KINGS 8:54

PRAYING FOR MY OWN NEEDS

Dear God, thank You for hearing the prayers I pray regarding my own needs. I often come to You exhausted and spent, sometimes not knowing which way to turn. It brings me great comfort that, in addition to praying for others, I may bring my burdens and requests to my loving, heavenly Father. I will seek You all the days of my life. You are able to do more than I can even ask or imagine. You can heal the broken parts of me. You can use me in spite of my inadequacies. Thank You, Lord. Amen.

441.

And call upon me in the day of trouble:
I will deliver thee, and thou shalt glorify me.

PSALM 50:15

442.

And the publican, standing afar off,
would not lift up so much as his eyes
unto heaven, but smote upon his breast,
saying, God be merciful to me a sinner.

LUKE 18:13

443.

For this thing I besought the Lord thrice,
that it might depart from me.

2 Corinthians 12:8

444.

Now unto him that is able to do exceeding
abundantly above all that we ask or think,
according to the power that worketh in us,
Unto him be glory in the church by Christ Jesus
throughout all ages, world without end. Amen.

Ephesians 3:20–21

445.

He went away again the second time, and prayed,
saying, O my Father, if this cup may not pass
away from me, except I drink it, thy will be done.

Matthew 26:42

446.

And the very God of peace sanctify you
wholly; and I pray God your whole spirit and
soul and body be preserved blameless unto
the coming of our Lord Jesus Christ. Faithful
is he that calleth you, who also will do it.

1 Thessalonians 5:23–24

447.

From the end of the earth will I cry unto
thee, when my heart is overwhelmed:
lead me to the rock that is higher than I.
For thou hast been a shelter for me,
and a strong tower from the enemy.

Psalm 61:2–3

448.

Have mercy upon me, O God, according to thy
lovingkindness: according unto the multitude of
thy tender mercies blot out my transgressions.

Psalm 51:1

449.

Delight thyself also in the LORD: and he
shall give thee the desires of thine heart.

PSALM 37:4

———————•·•·———————

450.

O remember not against us former iniquities:
let thy tender mercies speedily prevent us:
for we are brought very low.

PSALM 79:8

PRAYING FOR ENEMIES

Lord, it is easy to pray for those I love. But I know Your Word tells me to pray even for my enemies. Soften my heart, I ask, so that I may pray for my enemies to know You and to be blessed. I know that in doing so, I will grow in my faith as well. I may even rid myself of some anger or malice that lies beneath the surface in my heart. Guide me in how I should pray for those "difficult to love" people in my life. Amen.

451.

But I say unto you, Love your enemies,
bless them that curse you, do good to them
that hate you, and pray for them which
despitefully use you, and persecute you.

MATTHEW 5:44

452.

But I say unto you which hear, Love your
enemies, do good to them which hate you,
Bless them that curse you, and pray for
them which despitefully use you.

LUKE 6:27–28

453.

Blessed are ye, when men shall revile you,
and persecute you, and shall say all manner
of evil against you falsely, for my sake.
Rejoice, and be exceeding glad: for great is
your reward in heaven: for so persecuted
they the prophets which were before you.

MATTHEW 5:11–12

454.

Be not overcome of evil,
but overcome evil with good.

ROMANS 12:21

455.

Thou shalt not avenge, nor bear any grudge
against the children of thy people, but thou shalt
love thy neighbour as thyself: I am the LORD.

LEVITICUS 19:18

456.

But sanctify the Lord God in your hearts:
and be ready always to give an answer to
every man that asketh you a reason of the
hope that is in you with meekness and fear.

1 PETER 3:15

457.

Dearly beloved, avenge not yourselves,
but rather give place unto wrath: for it is written,
Vengeance is mine; I will repay, saith the Lord.

ROMANS 12:19

458.

Then said Jesus, Father, forgive them;
for they know not what they do.

LUKE 23:34

459.

Be ye therefore merciful, as your
Father also is merciful.

Luke 6:36

———————•◦•———————

460.

Forbearing one another, and forgiving one
another, if any man have a quarrel against any:
even as Christ forgave you, so also do ye.

Colossians 3:13

PRAYING THROUGH TRIALS

God, there are so many trials in life. It is easy to feel defeated. But as a believer, I have You on my side. If You are for me, who can be against me? Why should I fear? I know that You will see me through my current trials. And I can look back and see how You have delivered me before. Sometimes You calm the storm; and sometimes You simply carry me through it. Thank You for hearing my prayers and for growing my faith during times of trial. Amen.

461.

That the trial of your faith, being much more precious than of gold that perisheth, though it be tried with fire, might be found unto praise and honour and glory at the appearing of Jesus Christ.

1 PETER 1:7

462.

My brethren, count it all joy when ye fall into divers temptations; Knowing this, that the trying of your faith worketh patience. But let patience have her perfect work, that ye may be perfect and entire, wanting nothing.

JAMES 1:2–4

463.

For in that he himself hath suffered being tempted,
he is able to succour them that are tempted.

HEBREWS 2:18

464.

Blessed is the man that endureth temptation:
for when he is tried, he shall receive the crown
of life, which the Lord hath promised
to them that love him.

JAMES 1:12

465.

Rejoicing in hope; patient in tribulation;
continuing instant in prayer.

ROMANS 12:12

466.

And not only so, but we glory in tribulations also:
knowing that tribulation worketh patience.

ROMANS 5:3

467.

For I reckon that the sufferings of this present
time are not worthy to be compared with the
glory which shall be revealed in us.

ROMANS 8:18

468.

And we know that all things work together
for good to them that love God, to them who
are the called according to his purpose.

ROMANS 8:28

469.
Yea, and all that will live godly in
Christ Jesus shall suffer persecution.
2 TIMOTHY 3:12

———————•◦•———————

470.
I can do all things through Christ
which strengtheneth me.
PHILIPPIANS 4:13

PROBLEMS IN PRAYER

Heavenly Father, sometimes I don't know what to say when I pray. I struggle to believe You are really there and listening to me. I become distracted. I fall asleep. I lose focus. It is so frustrating that I have these problems praying. Please hear my heart even when the right words won't come. Show me, Father, that the important thing is that I make prayer a conversation with You and that I try. You are not looking for pretty words or perfectly formed thoughts. You just want me to commune with You daily in prayer. In Jesus' name I ask for Your help and guidance, amen.

471.

Humble yourselves therefore under the mighty hand of God, that he may exalt you in due time: Casting all your care upon him; for he careth for you.

1 Peter 5:6–7

472.

Ah Lord God! behold, thou hast made the heaven and the earth by thy great power and stretched out arm, and there is nothing too hard for thee.

Jeremiah 32:17

473.

Trust in the LORD with all thine heart;
and lean not unto thine own understanding.

PROVERBS 3:5

474.

These things I have spoken unto you, that
in me ye might have peace. In the world ye
shall have tribulation: but be of good cheer;
I have overcome the world.

JOHN 16:33

475.

He that searcheth the hearts knoweth
what is the mind of the Spirit, because
he maketh intercession for the saints
according to the will of God.

ROMANS 8:27

476.

Come unto me, all ye that labour and
are heavy laden, and I will give you rest.

MATTHEW 11:28

477.

But seek ye first the kingdom of God,
and his righteousness; and all these
things shall be added unto you.

MATTHEW 6:33

478.

Blessed is the man that endureth temptation:
for when he is tried, he shall receive
the crown of life, which the Lord hath
promised to them that love him.

JAMES 1:12

479.

Shew me thy ways, O Lord;
teach me thy paths.

Psalm 25:4

480.

Then hear thou from heaven thy dwelling
place, and forgive, and render unto every
man according unto all his ways, whose
heart thou knowest; (for thou only knowest
the hearts of the children of men).

2 Chronicles 6:30

PRAYERS FOR DELIVERANCE

Heavenly Father, I stand in need of deliverance. Deliver me, I pray, from sin and evil. Free me from depression and wrong thinking. I need rescue from that part of me that tends to dwell on the past. I have a new identity in Christ. And I am free! Deliver me from the temptation to live as though I am still a slave to sin and death. May I always seek You when I am in need of deliverance, for Your Word assures me that You stand ready to save Your own. Amen.

481.

Ye are of God, little children, and have overcome them: because greater is he that is in you, than he that is in the world.

1 John 4:4

482.

Stand fast therefore in the liberty wherewith Christ hath made us free, and be not entangled again with the yoke of bondage.

Galatians 5:1

483.

For whatsoever is born of God overcometh the world: and this is the victory that overcometh the world, even our faith. Who is he that overcometh the world, but he that believeth that Jesus is the Son of God?

1 John 5:4–5

484.

Thou art my hiding place; thou shalt preserve me from trouble; thou shalt compass me about with songs of deliverance.

Psalm 32:7

485.

Remember ye not the former things, neither consider the things of old. Behold, I will do a new thing; now it shall spring forth; shall ye not know it? I will even make a way in the wilderness, and rivers in the desert.

Isaiah 43:18–19

486.

Submit yourselves therefore to God.
Resist the devil, and he will flee from you.

JAMES 4:7

487.

Because he hath set his love upon me, therefore
will I deliver him: I will set him on high, because
he hath known my name. He shall call upon me,
and I will answer him: I will be with him in
trouble; I will deliver him, and honour him.

PSALM 91:14–15

488.

And it shall come to pass, that whosoever shall
call on the name of the LORD shall be delivered:
for in mount Zion and in Jerusalem shall be
deliverance, as the LORD hath said, and in the
remnant whom the LORD shall call.

JOEL 2:32

489.

Fear thou not; for I am with thee: be not
dismayed; for I am thy God: I will strengthen
thee; yea, I will help thee; yea, I will uphold
thee with the right hand of my righteousness.

Isaiah 41:10

490.

Then they cried unto the Lord in their trouble,
and he delivered them out of their distresses.

Psalm 107:6

PRAYING FOR MIRACLES

*Dear God, I read of the miracles in the Bible, and I
believe You can still work miracles today. Give me the
faith to pray big, not limiting You in any way. May my
endurance and patience in prayer, along with my faith,
increase as I pray for miracles. Whether I am asking for
healing or for a lost loved one to come to know You after
many years. . . . Regardless of the need I bring before
You, I will always believe in miracles. You are a
miracle-working God! Amen.*

491.

Verily, verily, I say unto you, He that believeth
on me, the works that I do shall he do also;
and greater works than these shall he do;
because I go unto my Father.

JOHN 14:12

492.

Thou art the God that doest wonders: thou hast
declared thy strength among the people.

PSALM 77:14

493.

So when this was done, others also, which had diseases in the island, came, and were healed.

ACTS 28:9

494.

And, behold, a woman, which was diseased with an issue of blood twelve years, came behind him, and touched the hem of his garment: For she said within herself, If I may but touch his garment, I shall be whole. But Jesus turned him about, and when he saw her, he said, Daughter, be of good comfort; thy faith hath made thee whole. And the woman was made whole from that hour.

MATTHEW 9:20–22

495.

And he saith unto them, Why are ye fearful, O ye of little faith? Then he arose, and rebuked the winds and the sea; and there was a great calm. But the men marvelled, saying, What manner of man is this, that even the winds and the sea obey him!

MATTHEW 8:26–27

496.

If ye have faith as a grain of mustard seed, ye shall say unto this mountain, Remove hence to yonder place; and it shall remove; and nothing shall be impossible unto you.

MATTHEW 17:20

497.

And they were all amazed, and spake among themselves, saying, What a word is this! for with authority and power he commandeth the unclean spirits, and they come out.

LUKE 4:36

498.

And Jesus looking upon them saith, With men it is impossible, but not with God: for with God all things are possible.

MARK 10:27

499.
God also bearing them witness,
both with signs and wonders, and
with divers miracles, and gifts of the
Holy Ghost, according to his own will?

HEBREWS 2:4

———— •◦• ————

500.
I will praise thee, O LORD, with my whole heart;
I will shew forth all thy marvellous works.

PSALM 9:1

PROMISES WOMEN
CAN COUNT ON. . .

The Bible Promise Book®:
500 Scriptures to Bless a Woman's Heart

Barbour's Bible Promise Books® are perennial
bestsellers, with millions of copies in print. The
Bible Promise Book® is available in a lovely
paperback edition featuring 500 scripture selections
plus encouraging prayer starters to bless women's
hearts. With 50 topics that matter most—including
Comfort, Love, Faith, Worry, Worship, Courage,
Joy, and Contentment—readers can quickly and
easily locate a topic that will speak to their needs.

Paperback / 978-1-68322-729-8 / $5.99

Find this and More from Barbour
Publishing at Your Favorite Bookstore
or at www.barbourbooks.com

BARBOUR
PUBLISHING